The Short Life of Free Georgia

The Short Life of Free Georgia

CLASS AND SLAVERY IN THE COLONIAL SOUTH

Noeleen McIlvenna

The University of North Carolina Press   Chapel Hill

Published with the assistance of the Fred W. Morrison Fund of the
University of North Carolina Press

Set in Miller by Westchester Publishing Services
Manufactured in the United States of America

The paper in this book meets the guidelines for permanence and
durability of the Committee on Production Guidelines for Book Longevity
of the Council on Library Resources. The University of North Carolina
Press has been a member of the Green Press Initiative since 2003.

Cover illustration: A view of Savanah [*sic*] as it stood the 29th of March, 1734,
engraving by P. Fourdrinier (Courtesy of Library of Congress, Prints and
Photographs Division, LC-USZC4-4715)

Complete cataloging information for this title is available
from the Library of Congress.
ISBN 978-1-4696-2403-7 (pbk.: alk. paper)
ISBN 978-1-4696-2404-4 (ebook)

THIS BOOK WAS DIGITALLY PRINTED.

For Maeve and Hugh

Contents

Figure and Maps

Acknowledgments

My gratitude goes to all the institutional support emanating from Wright State University. The Office of Research and Sponsored Programs provided two travel grants, and the College of Liberal Arts gave me additional funding for archival research and a year's leave to complete the writing. The librarians of Dunbar, especially Piper Martin, never lost patience with me. Fellow Writing Bootcampers ensured that writing was *not* the solitary activity scholars often bemoan. Colleagues from around the university endured alongside me as I slogged through volumes of Whitefield's letters and agonized over footnotes.

Fellow historians always improve the work. Peter Wood sent me boxes of books and ever-positive feedback throughout the long process. Alan Gallay read a portion and made it better. So, too, did Ava Chamberlain. Jonathan Bryant, and other readers for the press, sharpened the argument considerably. Librarians and archivists in Savannah, Athens, Charleston, Washington, D.C., and London seemed happy to help. The professionals at the University of North Carolina Press are a pleasure to work with.

Lance Greene generously helped with the maps, formatted the manuscript, read a chapter, and made the research travel possible. Tess Greene's fearlessness provided much-needed inspiration at times of ebbing confidence.

Maeve and Hugh will not see this book, but they shaped my thinking so much that they feature on every page.

In the end, it was the constant support and rallying from my writing group that allowed me to sustain the scholarship on a weekly basis for years. I looked forward to meeting them in classrooms, coffee shops, the library, and in their homes and mine. This project might have petered out at several different stages, but for them. Peggy Lindsey, Doug Lantry, and Lance Greene sat beside me at the beginning. Deborah Crusan, Carol Mejia Laperle, Sirisha Naidu, and Nimisha Patel signed up for the discipline and saw me over the finish line. Sarah Twill and Erin Flanagan were there the whole time. Rewarding me with fabulous prizes and, even better, fabulous company when I met my monthly goals, my Girl Mafia kept me laughing all the way. So it is all their fault if I made any errors.

The Short Life of Free Georgia

INTRODUCTION

> A story fruitful of Instruction to all the unfortunate Creatures who are
> oblig'd to seek their Re-establishment abroad; whether by the Misery of
> Transportation, or other Disaster; letting them know, that Diligence and
> Application have their due Encouragement, even in the remotest Parts of
> the World, and that no Case can be so low, so despicable, or so empty of
> Prospect, but that an unwearied Industry will go a great way to deliver us
> from it, will in time raise the meanest Creature to appear again in the
> World, and give him a new Cast for his Life.
> —Defoe, *Moll Flanders*

Daniel Defoe lived in London in the first decades of the eighteenth century
when the city boomed. As the population doubled between 1650 and 1750,
it seemed to the educated that crime and vagrancy had reached epidemic
levels. Defoe came to believe that transportation to the American colonies was the answer. This position stemmed not from a cruel instinct, but
a paternalistic worldview. A poor man, brought to crime by economic desperation, could start afresh with "a new Cast for his Life." *Moll Flanders*
promised prosperity to those who would sail west. With scant reference
to the difficulties of life in a thoroughly new world—Defoe made no mention of unwelcoming Indians or wholly foreign climatic conditions—Moll
will turn tragedy to triumph. By analogy, perhaps the impoverished and
the criminal might all find redemption in America.[1]

To fully understand the origins of Georgia, we must somehow let go of
what we know and travel back in time to a swampy forest. Before air-
conditioning and mosquito sprays, before the Civil War, even before cotton and rice plantations, German Pietists, Highland warriors, Lowland
gentry, and English servants set up a new society. They spent twenty years
fighting not for mere survival, although some days that alone seemed like
a victory. They argued over the future nature of Georgia. Some sought to
build a land of equal opportunity on a level playing field. Those with grit
and perseverance would prosper in such a spot, no matter their background. Others wanted to re-create what they left behind in Europe,
with a triangular social structure guaranteeing privileges only to the very

few at the top. When those few found out that Savannah's servants would not oblige them, they campaigned for permission to bring in those who could be physically forced to obey.

The colony of Georgia was founded in 1733, the last of the British colonies on the American mainland. The founders had a whole array of settlements from which to choose a model of governance, some in existence for over a century. Yet they tried something brand-new. Something like New England, in that it might be a symbol or example for others. Something like Pennsylvania, a safe place for persecuted German Protestants. Something like South Carolina, producing a new commodity for the Empire. Yet Georgia would essentially be better than all of those. It would be a wonderful philanthropic enterprise, driven not by greed, but by man's best impulses. At its core was a noblesse oblige idea: helping out the worthy poor by giving them a chance to work hard. The Trustees were not offering an opportunity to amass a fortune. They suggested only that disciplined agricultural labor might bring security from hunger and the crime it often provoked in London. In return for the free land, they expected obedience. However, once on that land, the poor dared snub their noses at the expectations of the rich.

We can only fully understand the narrative of the Trustee era when we grasp the world as they knew it. Southern history is too often presented in binary form: white versus black. Although race relations came to be the defining motif of the nineteenth and twentieth centuries, we should not cast that moral struggle back upon an era when it did not apply. In eighteenth-century England and its colonies abroad, social class separated people as surely as skin color would later. Social structure bore little resemblance to that of today. E. P. Thompson, the best scholar on the topic, breaks the country into two: patricians and plebeians. The patricians, or gentry, tended to have inherited their status, although there was some wiggle room for those who had made money in trade or the woolen industry to buy their way up. Critical to respectability was land ownership. On the crowded island, acreage signified status. The enclosure movement of the previous two centuries had consolidated estates, and the hedges separated the haves from the have-nots. The Church's role in social control diminished, but the theater of pomp—powdered wigs, hunting regalia, and of course the dialects of the upper crust—marked the authority of the top 5 percent.[2]

No substantial middle class we would recognize today would be seen in the early 1700s, although the second half of that century would see the emergence of an industrial and professional bourgeoisie who would struggle on either side of the Atlantic for some measure of power. But in the 1720s, that group still depended on the gentry's patronage to win appointments to places in the empire's bureaucracy.[3] They often echoed the gentry's complaints about the idleness of those beneath them.

Plebeians, or the laboring poor, constituted about 80 percent of England's population. Incorporating rural laborers, dispossessed peasants, craftsmen (many in the textile trade), and journeymen, we might also easily throw London's nascent proletariat into this group in terms of their income, status, or power. Gentlemen of the time certainly saw little difference. Lacking any financial security beyond the season, living from hand to mouth for their entire life span, most did whatever they felt necessary to survive. The first few decades of the eighteenth century saw less crowd action than other decades; the anti-enclosure movement had mostly waned, and food riots became a trend after 1740. But "in its resistance to religious homily, in its picaresque flouting of the provident bourgeois virtues, in its ready recourse to disorder, and in its ironic attitudes towards the Law," the plebeian class demonstrated it did not automatically defer to the higher-ups.[4]

Neither should we pretend that race had not been constructed as a divisive tool, to quell class antagonisms and set the poor against each other. South Carolina and Virginia planters were well under way with that manipulation, and the Georgia settlers of all classes had distinctly white supremacist attitudes toward the Africans they encountered in Atlantic ports. But race had not yet fully replaced class as the primary category of identity for the first generation.

This book attempts to tell the foundation story of Georgia from the political perspective of most of the first European settlers, not merely the few who came to dominate. Removed from England's normal social and political culture, where one's social class determined tight limits for one's possible future and demanded one's obedience to the upper ranks, poor settlers in Georgia refused to behave in the proper manner. As the philanthropic gentlemen failed in matters of management, the aura of their superiority evaporated. Then a couple of pastors preached about equality before God, and another chink in the wall of class customs came loose. As the servants stopped being servile, the planter gentlemen searched for a labor force that had no such choice. The 1750 end of the ban on slavery meant fewer opportunities for true economic mobility for poor white people. Planters grabbed all the best lands. And when the rich could force labor for no wages, why would they pay anyone? The planter class took over the economic and the political reins of the colony and exploited racism to prevent any potential class solidarity among those at the bottom. Most Georgians lost.

■ Colonial settlements represented ventures into the unknown for Europeans, largely unprepared for what awaited them as their boats pulled ashore. Georgia, though late in the timeline of European conquest in the Americas, still presented unforeseen challenges to those who risked everything in the dangerous Atlantic crossing. One of the most surprising elements of this narrative seems at first to be the naiveté of many of the players. How did both the Trustees and the settlers know so little about where they were going and what it would take to create the society they envisioned? Europeans had been visiting the region for nearly two hundred years. The British government and various private groups had established numerous colonies in the New World. Many lessons stood to be learned from those experiences, yet these first arrivals stumbled a great deal, repeating the seventeenth-century errors. They should have expected to face problems generating a new economy without infrastructure, to understand that a couple of decades would be spent figuring out what would work. They should have grasped that those early decades would see great hardship as malnutrition and disease took a toll, and that men would jockey for power. But the philanthropists chose to ignore history and assume they had invented a quick fix for poverty.

To give them credit, they anticipated certain problems. Western Georgia was home to the Creeks, who carefully chose the best locations to settle and hunt. The Lower Creeks by the eighteenth century had formed a coalescent community, having absorbed bands of people fractured by Old World diseases since Hernando de Soto and his men carried microbes across the Southeast. The Cherokees occupied northern Georgia.[5] By this time, the British imperial bureaucracy understood that Indian peoples would not be thrilled to declare themselves subjects to King George II, but that they would welcome a business relationship. The competition with the French for the allegiance of the Creeks necessitated a generous flow of European goods, which remained a priority throughout the 1730s and 1740s. An Indian delegation to England was met with dignity and hospitality, and the colony never endured Indian attack.

The Spanish were another matter. European statesmen liked clear territorial definitions with maps and boundary lines of latitude, and cited the legalities of treaties negotiated in the palaces of France. But in much the same way as American Indians, the realpolitik of weaponry made their borders no more permanent that those separating the Creek and Cherokee lands. The new colony, defined by the gap between English-controlled territory and that claimed by the Spanish, had enough overlap to cause a lot of friction in the early decades. Conflict came as no surprise, and the remnants of Georgia's early preparations for war can be seen at Fort Frederica on St. Simon's Island.

Yet the unforeseen threat to English plans for Georgia came not from foreigners whose aggression they anticipated, but from within the British colonies. The expansion-minded planters of South Carolina had different designs for the rice-friendly soils to their south, once James Oglethorpe had guaranteed safety from the Spanish. Their machinations caught the other groups involved off guard, and although Trustees and settlers alike reacted defensively, Charles Town's elite relentlessly stayed on offense.

■ For most of the immigrants the new life was tough, but then again, perhaps not as hard as the one they left behind, should they have been lucky enough to survive. Adaptation proceeded at different rates for different people. The tyranny of mortality kept most occupied with finding food and staying ahead of the fatal mosquito. Although most of the English women and men who came were urbanites, they tried farming, they built an orphanage, they served in the military, they traded for rum, and they hunted. The Highlanders raised cattle and fought the Spanish. German peasant farmers figured out how to grow crops in the new climate and built mills for processing lumber. Dragged periodically into a debate about slavery and the economy, the workers tried to figure out what best suited their needs.

Only when we look really closely at the actions of everyone can we paint the fullest portrayal of the colony. To do so requires that we work both our imagination and our reasoning. Regular people left scant records compared to the powerful, who not only created more documentation but were also more likely to preserve their paperwork. Thus it proves much easier for historians to tell their story. But in those same records, we can find the stories of others, even of the illiterate. Frustrated by laborers who demanded the market value of their labor, gentlemen railed against the gall of the servant class. And from those rants, we can piece together our picture, blurry at times of course, but a picture that contains more than those whose names are given to the streets and squares of Savannah.[6] The social historian must never take the words of the gentry at face value. We attempt to understand the full context of the remarks. Stand in the shoes of history's voiceless and imagine the story from their perspective. If a boss describes his workers as lazy or greedy, what would the workers say? Is it lazy to take breaks during six twelve-hour workdays under the southern August sun? Is it greedy to ask for a living wage after four years of unpaid indentured servitude? These questions are not meant to imply that every person born at the bottom of the social scale had a noble character of diligence and honor, but only to consider that they were at least as intelligent, hard-working, and honest as their employers.

However small in number they may be, the founding generation of any society hold a disproportionate influence on all those who follow because they set a pattern and a tone, fix the limits of the possible, and establish culturally sanctioned norms. Above all, the history of Georgia shows that the people who crossed the Atlantic in the eighteenth century carried visions for a new life that were not compatible with even their own shipmates' presumptions, let alone with the concept for a new society held by those who stayed in London. The first two decades witnessed a struggle to define Georgia: economically, socially, and religiously. That we know the result of their efforts now does not diminish the importance of an examination of how it became what it became. Much can be learned from the process of creation in the last British colony to be established and the last to join the thirteen in revolution.

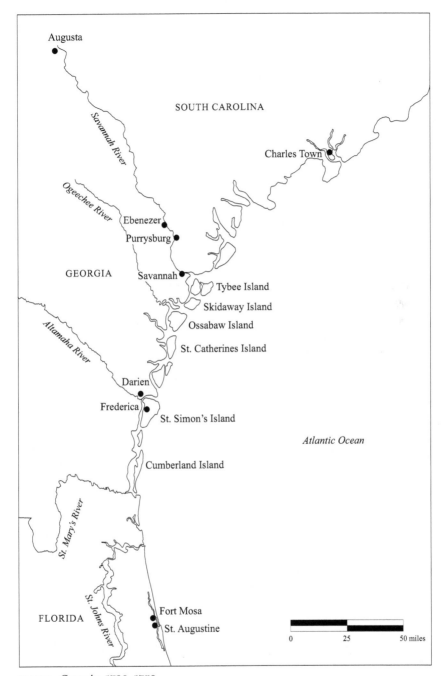

Augusta

SOUTH CAROLINA

Savannah River

Charles Town

Ogeechee River

Ebenezer
Purrysburg

GEORGIA   Savannah

Tybee Island

Skidaway Island

Ossabaw Island

St. Catherines Island

Altamaha River

Darien
Frederica

St. Simon's Island

Atlantic Ocean

Cumberland Island

St. Mary's River

St. Johns River

Fort Mosa

FLORIDA   St. Augustine

0   25   50 miles

MAP 1. *Georgia, 1730–1750*

1

PRE-GEORGIA, 1720s

I was carried to Newgate; that horrid Place! . . . the hellish Noise,
the Roaring, Swearing and Clamour, the Stench and Nastiness . . .
joyn'd together to make the Place seem an Emblem of Hell itself,
and a kind of an Entrance into it.
—Defoe, *Moll Flanders*

Daniel Defoe wrote the cautionary tale of Moll Flanders in 1722. Born to a whore in Newgate Jail, Moll lived a life of crime and debauchery as a prostitute and a thief until decades later, back in Newgate, she found God. Then she departed for the American colonies with her true love and started again, to "live as new People in a new World."[1] Defoe had spent three months imprisoned in Newgate. He understood that jails and workhouses rarely rehabilitated and that, in fact, they "too often make Reprobates" of debtors and those guilty of very minor offenses. Sobriety and hard work held the keys to redemption, both spiritual and material. And no better place existed for the poor to discover this truism for themselves than Britain's American colonies.[2]

Whether or not James Oglethorpe had read Defoe's novel we cannot know, but he certainly shared the idea that if England's poor could make their way across the Atlantic, they would find a spot to make their own Paradise by "unwearied Industry." At the end of the 1720s, Oglethorpe was the youngest son of a Jacobite-leaning family of the English landed gentry. After spending three years abroad on military service, he served as member of Parliament (MP) for the constituency of Haselmere in the south of England from 1722 on. In 1729 he chaired a committee charged with investigating "the State of the Gaols of this Kingdom," filled as they were with more debtors than felons. Oglethorpe compiled a "catalogue of corruption and cruelty" on the part of the prison officials, who accepted bribes from prisoners for better cells or facilitated escapes, while punishing others by confining them in smallpox-ridden dungeons.[3] His review resulted in little change in prison administrative practices, but around 10,000 debtors were released. Nothing improved in their financial affairs; they remained impoverished and might be destined to return to prison.

So Oglethorpe began discussions with philanthropists seeking a remedy. Another committee member, John Viscount Perceval, soon to become the Earl of Egmont, shared his sense of noblesse oblige. Together they hatched a very Enlightenment plan for progress: bringing order out of chaos, they would attain land in America where the worthy poor could work hard and get ahead.[4]

His widow being persued by the Creditors was forc'd to take Shelter in the Mint.
—Defoe, *Moll Flanders*

Oglethorpe's endeavor should be seen in the context of the attitudes prevailing among the governing class toward the poor and unemployed during the 1720s. Moll Flanders met other debtors in the Mint, a neighborhood on the south side of the Thames that had served as a sanctuary for debtors in the seventeenth century. But in 1723 an act of Parliament shut off that avenue. The very first workhouse had been built in 1697, and a further piece of legislation in 1723, the Knatchbull Act, showed how the gentry loved this idea, for it provided for a nationwide extension of these institutions, where the poor could be supervised to ensure they worked hard enough to earn their keep.[5] Disdainful of the slightest hint of idleness amongst the paupers, schemes to keep them industrious became quite the fashion among the London set.

He . . . talk'd as naturally of his Park and his Stables, of his Horses, his Game-Keepers, his Woods, his Tenants, and his Servants, as if we had been in the Mansion-House.
—Defoe, *Moll Flanders*

One more act should be noted. Passed by Parliament in 1723, the Black Act (9 George I c. 22) marked a new departure for English law. Throughout the seventeenth century, peasants had rioted or fought in courts to prevent or limit the huge drainage schemes in eastern England's fens. The investors in such schemes assumed ownership of the lands, robbing many from their livelihoods. By the early eighteenth century, the English agricultural poor lost further ground to deer parks. The Black Act made fifty offenses of hunting, fishing and poaching in royal and private forests capital crimes. Designed apparently to quell the Waltham Blacks, people who masked their faces as they stole royal deer, the severity of the law seems difficult to explain given that only a couple of incidents provoked its passage. Yet, from that date on, the poor of Britain found themselves shut out from what many had previously assumed were common lands and common game. Guilty parties were imprisoned, transported to the colonies, or executed.[6]

Struggle for control of some forests' resources had been waged between official gamekeepers and local residents of every class. Deer, although the chief prize, constituted only a portion of the valuable commodities the huge parks offered. Timber and peat provided heat in the winter, and farmers liked to graze hogs, sheep, and cattle upon areas of open ground. But Windsor Forest's primary purpose was to afford the king his leisure. George I, recently arrived from Germany and a sportsman, liked his parks well stocked. The custom had been, however, that people who lived in or around the periphery of any forest could enjoy some of its fruits, including deer who had escaped the fenced areas. Common-law precedents from centuries past granted these rights to both copyholders (tenants) and freeholders, but at the turn of the eighteenth century, court decisions increasingly went in favor of the large landholders. As the nobility followed the fashion for landscaping and creating pleasure parklands out of their manor grounds, they instituted this program of tighter enforcement of forest law. Outraged local plebeians responded with organized attacks in 1720 and 1722. These attacks went beyond stealing food. The foresters made a political statement, claiming common rights and threatening nobles with retribution. "They would at a convenient season balance accounts with him, and leave not a stick standing in his park or house," some Waltham Blacks warned an encroaching Earl.[7]

The 1723 Black Act brought the hammer down. It would supersede all the customary freedoms, pushing regular folk out of the forest. "*Liberty* and *Forest Laws* are incompatible," commented one contemporary.[8] Aristocratic privilege would be extended. The deer required a wide range of undisturbed property to thrive, and their needs outranked those of the human inhabitants. One did not have to kill a deer to warrant execution. Cutting turf or peat disrupted the deer habitat; the punishment was hanging. Fishing from private ponds became a capital crime. Aiding or abetting the accused also brought the death sentence. The brutality of this repression highlights the new esteem for private property, offenses against which rivaled those against person.

The Black Act carries great significance for the early decades of English settlement in the colony of Georgia for several reasons. First, the act stands as a marker of the "elevation of property above all other values," as elite Whigs under Prime Minister Robert Walpole drew boundary lines around liberties and completed the two-century process of the enclosure of common lands. Second, as E. P. Thompson argues, both the joys of hunting and the venison such a pursuit produced became exclusive to the highest levels of society. Venison "was a sign of status, and the gift of game was one of the more delicate means by which the gentry expressed influence." For anyone from the lower orders to partake represented not merely a quest for free meat, but a gesture of defiance against the rigid social hierarchy in Britain. Third, the enforcement of the act reminds us that definitions of rural and urban apply differently to the eighteenth century, for accused Waltham Blacks were not necessarily farmers. Often skilled artisans, such as wheelwrights, blacksmiths and bakers, they had also learned to operate a crossbow.[9] Fourth, as the legal apparatus swung even more lopsidedly in favor of the richest few, the only power remaining in the hands of those at the bottom was that which they could wield as a juror. Thompson tells the story of John Huntridge, charged with harboring a deer stealer, but acquitted by a jury who understood his case to have been influenced by Walpole himself.[10] In Georgia, far removed from the repressive infrastructure of England's courts, activist juries would happily exercise their right to acquit those obviously guilty under unjust laws.

Before their executions, the condemned poachers were "almost poysoned" in jail, a place "very full and noisome and overrun with excrement," according to its inhabitants.[11] There they would encounter debtors, locked up in such savage prisons only for want of a more generous line of credit, as well as any English persons who dared publicly berate their government and might be suspected of Jacobitism.[12] Oglethorpe, serving as an inspector of the Fleet and Marshalsea prisons, institutions specifically for debtors in the late 1720s, was so horrified by conditions that he launched a successful campaign to secure the release of the insolvent.[13] Their liberation, however welcome, was not accompanied by any financial relief, and thus Oglethorpe spearheaded the drive for a colony in the New World that would provide a fresh start. In the end, Georgia was not a debtor colony; the Trustees did not recruit debtors, but those they considered the worthy poor, who would be joined later by others who had served time in English jails and were all too aware of the limitations on the use of English forests.

Over the course of 1730 and 1731, Oglethorpe and Egmont recruited supporters and raised funds, including a legacy from the estate of Rev. Thomas Bray, head of the Society for the Propagation of the Gospel, a Church of England missionary organization for the American colonies. With further discussion, the idea evolved into creating a colony for the

English poor and persecuted European Protestants in the region between South Carolina and Florida. As an object of competing claims from European powers, this area would be a buffer zone that protected the English colonies from Spanish interference, and thus would require a military component. Oglethorpe believed his military experience sufficient to enable him to command any mission against Spanish aggression. The philanthropists applied to the Privy Council for a land grant and charter in September 1731.

Such a colony demanded heavy financing, and the group hoped to raise most from private sources. A publicity campaign reached towns the length and breadth of Britain, with tracts describing the area in glowing terms. But too many investors had been burned by losses in earlier similar ventures. Despite their best efforts, it rapidly became apparent that government support was crucial. To sell the concept to the king and to Parliament, the planners promised that this colony, to be named after George I, would benefit not merely the impoverished, but the kingdom back home. It would clean London streets of thousands of those filthy poor, such a "Burthen on their Parishes"; it would keep the Spanish from preying on the riches of South Carolina, and they would grow silk to free England of its dependency on foreign sources.[14] Some influential merchants of London picked up their ears at this latter commercial possibility and endorsed the plan, joining the Board of Trustees in 1733.[15] The king agreed and granted them a charter for a nonprofit colony in the land between the Savannah and Altamaha Rivers, to take effect in June 1732. The trust was incorporated to run a new "charitable" colony named Georgia for twenty-one years. Over one-half of the original Trustees also sat in Parliament, but the House of Commons rejected the initial petition for funds to launch the endeavor. Many seemed concerned that Georgia would drain England of the unemployed, perhaps worrying that wages might rise in consequence. The MPs agreed to examine the request for money again later, but for the first year, the onus lay with the Trustees to collect the necessary funding through their public appeals.[16] They would also try harder to recruit oppressed European Protestants. Parliament more happily supported relief for Germans than for their brother Englishmen, assuming those who would suffer for their Protestantism would be driven by a work ethic to honor God. Once Parliament began to support the endeavor financially, they did so through grants issued or renewed each year (rather than an automatic payment) so that the development of Georgia would be on the annual agenda and open to debate.

Oglethorpe tried to comfort those who feared the loss of production in England by comparing Protestant England to the Catholic powers. "They have in each of those Kingdoms more than One Hundred Thousand Cloyster'd Females, not permitted to propagate their Species, and the Number of Males in a State of Celibacy is still abundantly greater . . . It may be said indeed, that these don't marry, yet many of them get Children. But it must be admitted that the usual Fate of that Kind of Propagation is to be destroyed secretly, either before or after the Birth; and the Former of these Crimes frequently procures Barrenness in the Woman." Britons held Catholics in low esteem in the eighteenth century. Oglethorpe computed the effects of Catholic celibate orders and their secret fertility-destroying abortions upon the French and Spanish populations and concluded that England could "afford to send People Abroad better."[17] There was absolutely no evidence for his assertion about nuns. But Parliamentarians remained unconvinced about letting workers leave England, and so to win funding, the Trustees turned to the beleaguered Pietists of Salzburgh in southwestern Germany and offered them a sanctuary in Georgia.

To the Trustees, the chief purpose of their enterprise entailed the uplifting of the downtrodden, and the rules they crafted for the colony reflected that goal. With alcoholic spirits forbidden, they designed land-tenure regulations to prevent the amassing of huge plantations or estates, and most firmly held of all, the use of slaves was absolutely prohibited. All these measures should avert "idleness and vice in the people," the biggest risk to the success of the colony. Government would come from England, with trust officials in Savannah acting as employees, rather than executives, for there would be no governor.[18]

Land would be granted free of charge, but under strict rules. The regulations governing ownership of land stemmed from the goals of the Trustees. No individual might own more than 500 acres. They did not have the freedom to sell or to mortgage their land; if they left, the property would revert to the trust. A further restriction, known as "tail-male tenure," prohibited all women from inheriting land, to prevent anyone consolidating large plantations through a series of marriages. If only women survived, the land reverted back to the trust so that it could be granted to a man. The Trustees justified these limitations by explaining that anyone released from debtor's prison had shown themselves to be less than sensible in the management of their English property, and so must prove through "careful and industrious behavior" that they were trustworthy.

The benevolence accorded them by the British public in paying for their voyage, their resources, and their upkeep was an investment, and the British public really "owned" the land until the charity colonists had earned it through hard work. It seemed crucial, too, that the colony attract enough white men to ensure military security from Spain.[19]

Even those who financed their own passage across the Atlantic, the "gentlemen" who would be granted the large 500-acre lots, must abide by the same tenure restrictions. In addition, these private entrepreneurs must bring male servants, one for every fifty acres, and clear and cultivate at least 100 acres within ten years of arrival. They were also obliged to plant a thousand mulberry trees on their lands to promote the silk industry. But once in Georgia, men who paid their own way declined to consider themselves under any obligation for the free land granted them.

The prohibition of rum had been suggested in an earlier colonial proposal by Thomas Coram, one of the Trustees. Coram had spent time in Massachusetts and credited the outbreak of King Phillip's War in the 1670s to alcohol. Indians had been plied with spirits and then defrauded of their land; in anger they had attacked the New England settlements.[20] Blame for the more recent Yamasee War in South Carolina also lay with the role played by liquor in the cheating of Indians. In addition, many believed that alcohol and the poor made for a bad mix. Once Oglethorpe landed in Georgia, he concluded that the climate combined with rum to bring fevers and death to settlers. Taken together, these factors led the Trustees beyond their original management regulation into the passing of permanent legislation, with a 1735 Act banning the importation or consumption of rum in the colony.[21] Unfortunately, this did not aid commerce, as Caribbean rum functioned almost as currency, such was its importance in the Atlantic commodity trade.

Of all the regulatory aspects of the Trustees' design, the prohibition of slavery proved the most controversial. In the ensuing decades, settlers successfully protested the land-tenure restrictions and paid no heed to the ban on rum. But the Trustees held their ground when would-be planters sent ardent claims that Georgia must fail without slaves, and their reasons must be understood. The English philanthropists opposed slavery *not* on behalf of Africans, but because the "peculiar institution" would undercut the very raison d'etre of the colony: the salvation of the English poor through labor. Were slavery allowed, "they would be unwilling, nay would certainly disdain, to work like negroes," argued the Trustees, and so their moral compass would be lost.[22] As Betty Wood has explained, the Trustees should not be considered abolitionists or even pre-abolitionists, although a couple of their arguments were later picked up by those groups.[23] The snobbery inherent in the attitudes of the philanthropists seemed entirely normal and appropriate in eighteenth-century England; hard work in the fields was not only necessary but good for those at the bottom, while their social betters diverted themselves hunting and fishing in kid gloves that kept their hands soft and white.

Perhaps many among the English poor accepted the limits of the possible in England, but the Waltham Blacks fought the increase of elite control, and did the rest really buy into the premises upon which their social order was constructed? Just a few generations before, Oliver Cromwell's New Model Army, based on promotion by merit, had overthrown the monarchy and House of Lords. Now Walpole's Home Office invested much greater proportions of the public Treasury on state repression through spies, prisons, and policemen. The extent of the deference of London's working class would face a test in the Georgia wilderness, where no state infrastructure could enforce the king's laws or the Trustees' rules.

For any unmoved by the plight of the poor, the Trustees provided other motivations for the founding of Georgia at the public expense. "We shall . . . have the Navigation and Dominion of the Ocean establish'd in us more firmly than ever," claimed Oglethorpe, insinuating that the Royal Navy would secure a strategically important port from which to keep close watch over Spanish treasure fleets. "Great Britain will then be able to sell Silk Manufactures cheaper than all Europe," he went on, for the climate and soils of the region apparently lent themselves to the easy care of silk worms and mulberry trees. Supposedly, both the future farmers of Georgia and the textile manufacturers in England would grow rich as the French and Italian silk industry declined as a result of the competition.[24]

For many parliamentarians, the strongest argument for financing a colony in Georgia was the creation of a defensive block to Spanish aggression. Any tourist who first explores Puerto Rico's majestic Castillos, San Cristobal, and San Felipe del Morro, and then compares the architecture of Virginia's Colonial Williamsburg begins to comprehend the relative power of the British and Spanish Empires in the Americas. Although the power of the Spanish Empire was not in 1730 what it had been in 1530 or even 1630, the Spanish had occupied St. Augustine for almost two centuries and felt they had a legitimate claim on the lands to the north, for the British signed away their claims to all territory south of Charleston in 1690. The Spanish had never made any profit from Florida, however; it fulfilled only strategic and defensive roles. Whitehall's jealousies of and hostilities with the territorially ambitious Philip V of Spain continued to fester through the 1720s, with Britain failing in its attempt to blockade Porto Bello and the Spanish rebuffed at Gibraltar. Such was the context of the Georgia Charter.[25]

■ Everyone involved in the enterprise seemed convinced that Georgia's place on the globe made it "one of the most delightful countries in the universe!" Jean Pierre Purry, who would lead Swiss and Germans to settle just on the other side of the line in Carolina, boasted "no region in France, in Spain, in Italy" could compete with the natural beauty of the area.[26] Certainly St. Simon's Island was a gorgeous spot, but when planting food to sustain life, let alone producing enough for an export crop, the experienced farmer will hardly seek out sand. The coastal plain of Georgia is composed primarily of pine barrens and wetlands. Swamps and marshes are waterlogged terrain, perfect for rice if little else, and rice cultivation demands "especially elaborate manipulations of the environment," not feasible for the poorer settlers. Sandy soils in the pine barrens could support pine trees and oaks too, but would not deliver high yields of wheat or root crops without heavy fertilization, although Indian corn would grow. Even with a benevolent climate of plentiful rain and sun and a ten-month growing season, the first colonists struggled to locate enough of the occasional patches of rich soil that would render the bountiful harvests the promotional literature had guaranteed.[27]

If the land lacked the nutrients humans sought, it did not disappoint other forms of life. By the 1720s, Georgia's forests teemed not only with deer but also with wild cattle, descendants of escapees from the Spanish herds of Florida and from South Carolina's cattle ranches. These feral animals lived on the abundant cane of the wetlands, and their numbers would swell with the colonists' imported livestock, for early settlers had trouble containing their cattle. Hogs would soon join the livestock tasting freedom. A fisherman's paradise, the Savannah River hosted schools of herring, bass, catfish, sturgeon, and shad passing through to spawn. Feeding on smaller fish, flocks of ducks and geese of many species found pleasant habitats along the rivers and streams, but the very fattest birds were the wild turkeys. Mouth-watering crabs and clams lived along the intracoastal waterway. Not all the wildlife tempted the taste buds, however. Nearby hid snakes, wolves, and alligators.[28] Mosquitoes, "noctious Insects that sufficiently plague us in the summer," tortured the Englishmen.[29]

The natural flora offered some nutrition, with berries and nuts of all kinds available to any person or black bear who would gather them. Sweet potatoes were a new flavor to the European immigrants, although they had certain drawbacks. "For heavy workers it is a good, tasty, quickly prepared and nutritious food," commented one of the first Germans to settle in Georgia, "but," he warned, "delicate people who lead a sedentary life suffer from much wind through it."[30] Perhaps white southerners' common desire to keep a little space between themselves and their neighbors sprang from this early dietary regime. The dense and seemingly endless forests astonished British travelers most—and lit up the eyes of merchants. Shipbuilders and coopers alike wanted to harvest giant bald cypress and live oak lumber. The Royal Navy and the merchant marine needed naval stores like pitch and tar from the pine trees. For nonentrepreneurial types, the forest held less appeal. The huge magnolias' sweet scent was the original southern charmer, while palmettos welcomed overheated walkers with shade, but they stood in the way of planting crops.[31]

Overheated might be an understatement. Although short mild winters appealed to Londoners, the intensity of the summer heat, reaching ninety degrees most days, felt unbearable to arrivals from northern Europe; high humidity made the very idea of physical activity draining. Sticky, sweaty colonial-era settlers throughout the southern colonies blamed their high mortality rates on fevers and swelling brought on by the climate. Compounding a poor diet, malaria, scurvy, and dysentery from drinking the brackish waters were more likely culprits, we know now. Indeed, one environmental historian reminds us that "mosquitoes and viruses infringe on the fortunes of humankind in ways that seem unflattering to our species, making us seem mere playthings in dramas wrought (not directed) by tiny mindless creatures."[32] So it would be in 1730s Georgia, as Europeans succumbed in huge numbers to malaria, without any understanding of why they suffered. Poor nutrition always exacerbated illness; crop storage in prerefrigeration times posed an unsolvable problem, as the heat and worms prevented any stocking of surplus.[33]

While the gentlemen of England pursued their version of humanitarian reform, in Charles Town, men well used to the climate and who had discovered how to render the soils very lucrative looked to Georgia as a fresh field to conquer. Charles Town was originally settled in the 1670s; South Carolina's planters had discovered the enormous profitability of rice and, having forced their African slaves to bring much of their colony's swampy coastline under cultivation, turned their thoughts toward expansion. The planters had developed a plantation complex with slave labor, both Indian and African, where a few might amass extraordinary wealth and live like the aristocracy of Britain. "An incorrigible and politically corrupt elite" were prepared to take whatever steps necessary to expand their power and their economic regime.[34]

The Yamasee War of 1715 put an end to the trade in Indian slaves. Enslaved Africans, first brought to Carolina by the Barbadians in 1671, outnumbered white settlers by 1708, and the colony reminded visitors more of the Caribbean sugar colonies than any of its mainland neighbors. Charles Town, by 1720 North America's major slave port, attracted ships directly from Africa. The British had taken over the Atlantic slave trade by the early eighteenth century and transported nearly 10,000 slaves to the mainland colonies in the 1720s.[35] These stolen people endured the barbarities of the Middle Passage and the shocking humiliation of the auction block before finding themselves on a rice plantation surrounded by foreigners.

Rice flourished in the climate and marshy soils of the region. No English farmer had any familiarity with its husbandry, but the New World would encourage them to combine seeds and farming techniques from around the world to make South Carolina the richest of all the mainland colonies in the eighteenth century. The production of indigo and naval stores later supplemented the planters' income, but it was slave-grown and slave-processed rice that would build South Carolina. "This country is not capable of being cultivated by white men . . . Negroes are to this country what raw materials are to another country," claimed one leading planter.[36] They altered the perception of valuable land; rice grew in what had been considered at first as swampy wasteland.

Slaves cleared the freshwater swamp fields of vegetation, then constructed an earthen dam to control irrigation. Seeds were planted in the spring, hoed regularly in the early summer by laborers constantly stooped over, irrigated all summer and harvested in the fall. Tons of rice had then to be threshed with flails and pounded by hand with mortar and pestle, like the African practice, but the enormous quantities produced on the plantation made this exhausting task often fatal. Only the ever-present threat and reality of torture could keep the plantation producing at the levels demanded by the masters. The Low Country meant a short life expectancy. The harsh working conditions took such a toll that, unlike in Virginia, the slave population could not reproduce itself. But output doubled in the 1720s and again in the 1730s. South Carolina exported almost 5,000 tons of rice in 1726.[37]

For the masters, the rewards were lavish, and aspects of the culture of conspicuous consumption that developed would seem familiar to us. "The splendor, lust, and opulence there has grown almost to the limit. If the family did not go along with it, it would be despised," observed a minister acquainted with 1730s Charles Town. Any who wished social acceptance would have to keep up with "the often changing Charlestown fashion," he continued. "Otherwise there would be much humiliation and mockery." The pressure to maintain the facade drove many to poor decisions. "After the death of great gentlemen particularly, one hears that with all their pomp they had been deep in debt."[38] Planters driven by their material desires cared little for humanitarian goals. They craved new lands, ready for timbering and rice.

North Carolina seemed the most obvious area for expansion. The Moores, known simply as "The Family," began the process in 1725, marrying into one of North Carolina's planter families and befriending the new governor to get around proprietary restrictions on land grants in the Lower Cape Fear region, just across the border from South Carolina. Establishing the town of Brunswick, Maurice and his brother Roger Moore soon imported hundreds of enslaved people into the region and claimed headright land (a grant of fifty acres per person) for each of them. Although residents of North Carolina moved south into the new area too, it was the South Carolinian contingent whose economic and political ideology would dominate not just Cape Fear, but within a generation, most of North Carolina. Eight former South Carolinians who moved north before 1731 came to hold more than 91,000 acres. Onto this land they brought a "vast number of Negroes," according to one visitor to the area, and set up slave labor camps. Rice would not grow in the Cape Fear region, however, and the planters devoted their slaves to the profitable industry of naval stores production. For the more satisfying rice soils, the Carolinians would look south to the marshes of Georgia.[39]

One great antagonism to the Carolinian planters was the existence of an escape route for runaway slaves. Florida had been their destination since the late seventeenth century and officially became a sanctuary in 1693, when the Spanish Crown offered freedom to any who escaped the British Empire. In 1702, James Moore led a force largely composed of Indian allies to St. Augustine, where he futilely bombarded the Castillo de San Marcos. When the Spanish mustered extra help from Cuba, Moore abandoned his mission and fled. Back home, the Assembly let him feel their displeasure, and to restore his reputation, Moore gathered another self-financed military force composed primarily of Yamasee warriors the following year. This much more successful expedition focused on Apalache, the northwestern section of Spanish Florida. Moore's men destroyed the Franciscan missions, capturing booty in the form of both church silver and thousands of Indian slaves. Florida's Indian population sank by two-thirds in the following decade as a result. The Spanish described the area as "wholly laid waste being destroyed by the Carolinians," and their hold on north Florida was seriously reduced. Charles Town rebuffed an attack by a combined Spanish and French force in 1706, securing peace for two decades. In the meantime, the population of South Carolina, both black and white, soared, while the region separating them from Florida was largely abandoned by Indians.[40] St. Augustine remained secure, however, and escaping slaves continued to find a way there. After the Yamasee War of 1715, ex-slaves and Yamasees driven out of Carolina mounted joint raids on outlying plantations, freeing other slaves. An all-black militia would defend St. Augustine against Carolinian counterattacks in the 1720s.[41]

In 1733, the Spanish king publicized again the offer of emancipation to any slave who could make it through the swampy jungle between Carolina and Florida. The Carolinians badly wanted to shut off this path. So at first, they encouraged the development of the new colony. White settlement in Georgia would mean a buffer zone and extra slave patrols, adding difficulty to the labyrinthine route those seeking to own themselves had to navigate. However, they did not anticipate the Trustees' prohibition of slavery and quickly the attitude of Charles Town residents toward Georgia grew hostile. Instead, they encouraged a Swiss adventurer named Jean Pierre Purry to organize an asylum for persecuted Protestants on the South Carolina side of the Savannah River, for "the protection of lowcountry planters from threats real and imagined."[42] This settlement named Purrysburg provides an interesting comparative case study for Georgia, as it evolved under the auspices of South Carolina's Assembly. Compared to the Georgia Trustees, Carolina's government placed few legal restrictions on new arrivals.

■ The region that would become Georgia actually belonged not to any European monarch, but to the Creek Indians, although few settled in the area around Savannah. Clustered along the Alabama and Chattahoochee Rivers, Upper and Lower Creeks assigned sovereignty to each town, a localized control type of governance. Exposure to European diseases reduced the population but not so much that they could not present an imposing martial force. Through their cooperation in the attacks of the Yamasee War, the Lower Creeks helped bring an end to the Indian slave trade.[43] The Yamasees fled to St. Augustine after their defeat in 1715 and continued to raid plantations on the southern edge of South Carolina. But by the 1720s, the Lower Creeks had again negotiated an economic and military alliance with the British. One small group, the Yamacraws, a blend of Creek and Yamasee kin, could not choose between their relatives and moved off to the coast in 1728. Led by Chief Tomochichi, this band of kinsfolk established a new village, just a few years before the arrival of the first Georgia colonists.[44]

The Yamacraw, after many decades of European contact, mixed features of Creek, Yamasee, and English culture. They still wore less clothing overall than Europeans, given their climate, but did dress in English breeches and petticoats. Guns and ammunition held the most value of all English goods, whereas pots and pans were handy additions to the home. These items enhanced Indian ways of life, making hunting more effective, for example, but had radically changed neither their customs nor their political structures. Sharing a tobacco pipe continued to mark the opening of diplomatic councils, attended by many men from the small village, not solely Tomochichi.[45] Twenty years later, the Europeans understood Indian egalitarian power relations better. "It may be said and written that they have kings, but they are nothing except chiefs in war, namely the most courageous and daring, also possibly the most reasonable. Otherwise they cannot order the other Indians around."[46]

To prospective settlers and philanthropists, Oglethorpe portrayed the Indians of Georgia as lesser and grateful business partners of the British. Yet there should be no doubt as to his attitude toward anyone less white than himself. He cited the British colonization of Ireland to show that the Trustees had studied and learned from others' errors. Unlike early attempts to conquer Ireland, which had failed as a result of "mixing and intermarrying" with locals and thus degeneration, Georgia's Trustees would look to the later Plantation of Ulster. Places like Londonderry and Coleraine provided a wonderful precedent, claimed Oglethorpe, as "no other Part of Ireland is now so perfectly free from the native Irish."[47] Yet he understood the balance of power that would face the earliest settlers in Savannah and managed to contain or mask his English supremacy well enough to forge a positive relationship with the natives of Georgia. Before the *Anne* had anchored in Savannah, he would seek out Tomochichi and negotiate a site for the colony's first town.

Ostracized from his fellow Creeks, Tomochichi from the beginning needed allies and had land to spare. He arranged a formal greeting for the settlers on February 1, 1733, with a welcome ceremony that incorporated both Indian and English traditions and with interpreters clearly comfortable communicating in English. Little about the newcomers surprised the Indians, accustomed as they were to traders, whereas most of the arrivals must have found everything bizarre. Oglethorpe had been abroad before, and therefore accommodated the strange behaviors more readily. Some of his English supremacist thinking, however, is revealed in his description of the day's events in a letter back to the Trustees. According to his reading of the proceedings, Tomochichi and his brethren "desire[d] to be subject of the Trustees."[48] Gradually, European settlers would understand that Indians had never agreed to be "subjects of the English, but consider themselves noblemen and allies of the English."[49]

Loaded, then, with more cultural than material baggage, the new inhabitants of Georgia embarked on an experimental society. A wide range of unvoiced expectations and aspirations filled their thoughts and guided their actions over the next decade. A gulf in desires opened not merely between colonists in America and the Trustees in England, but also between classes of colonists. Georgia was settled by British-born, and anyone born in Britain in the eighteenth century understood very clearly where they ranked socially. Class antagonisms and aggression were little disguised at home and obviously could not magically evaporate on a transatlantic voyage. We know the history of Georgia from the vantage point of race. Let us now examine it through the lens of class and see how the traditional story changes.

2

WORKERS, 1733–1736

They meant one Sort of thing, by the Word Gentlewoman, and I meant
quite another. . . . All I understood by being a Gentlewoman, was to be able
to Work for myself, and get enough to keep me without that terrible Bug-
bear going to Service, whereas they meant to live Great, Rich, and High.
—Defoe, *Moll Flanders*

Defoe gave voice to the dreams of many, when he had Moll confuse gentlewoman status with autonomy: to live out one's days without constant
critical supervision. "The main process of the narrative is Moll's convo-
luted and twisting search for comfort and security," writes one literature
scholar.[1] But she could not find that security legitimately in England, so
she resorted to prostitution and thievery. To the horror of the aristocrats
in London and those who hoped to be aristocrats in Savannah, the new
Georgians, like Moll in England, resisted any attempt to keep them servile. So the first three years of settlement in Georgia did not play out quite
the way the Trustees envisioned. As poor people arrived from England and
Germany, they discovered a hot, steamy world of sickness and spent 1733
watching in dismay as their family members died in front of their eyes,
their crops failed, and the magistrates inflicted severe punishment on any
misbehavior. But as they gradually understood their collective power so
far from the legal infrastructures, workers, free and indentured, began to
assert themselves.

When we define a colony as "successful" (and no writers have used
that word to describe 1730s Georgia), we have to consider definitions of
success—are they necessarily economic measurements? Can we quantify
all factors of quality of life, such as the value of personal autonomy or even
climatic conditions? And if we do concentrate on the economic, how do we
ascertain the goals of these arrivals? Historians of early America quarrel
whether seventeenth- and eighteenth-century colonists sought a "competency," a comfortable subsistence, or "profit maximization," the fully
formed capitalist aspiration we are conscious of today. The young Moll certainly leaned toward the former; anything but being a servant. Probably,
people left England's shores dreaming of a better life for themselves and

their children. But to figure out what "better than servant life in eighteenth-century England" means we need to have some sense of their lives at home.

We can best sum up the 1600s as a century of dispossession for England's peasants. Just as the population soared, the landed gentry used enclosures of agricultural land to mold those peasants into wage laborers. Enclosure meant the construction of high hedges to keep sheep confined as the British wool industry developed. It also meant that peasants who had worked those fields for their own food supply for generations suddenly found themselves without any land. The insecurity of employment in a preindustrial economy led to great numbers of poverty-stricken individuals and a majority who lived on the brink. Young landless men and women might go into domestic service or work in agriculture. Servants-in-husbandry in England tended to be single eighteen- to twenty-five-year-olds. They signed one-year contracts with their masters and lived as a family member in the household. But when they could find no contracts, they drifted toward London in search of employment and found whatever way they could to survive. The potential social and political consequences of this explosion of young landless men terrified the ruling class who had created them, and one solution was to pack them off to the colonies in the Caribbean or American mainland.[2]

The plans for Georgia were only the latest rendering of a system suggested by George Peckham in 1583. "There is at this day great numbers . . . which live in such penurie & want, as they could be contented to hazarde their lives, and to serve one yeere for meat, drinke, and apparel, onely without wages, in hope thereby to amend theyr estates."[3] The indenture system in the Americas, however, tied them for an average term of four years *without any pay*, and at any point the remainder of that term might be sold without their consent. Certainly, they received their room, board, and clothing—expenses their employer might regard as a type of wage—but they had no control over their own labor. It was not unusual for anyone from the age of thirteen on to be sent to America, and minors normally served throughout their teenage years until their early twenties. Judges guessed the age for some helpless, undocumented teens—those without indentures—and might sentence them to long terms. As the system evolved over the seventeenth century, American masters rarely regarded their servants as family.[4] Ample opportunity for horrible exploitation of the young meant that abuse was widespread.

The baggage stowed on the Atlantic crossing included the customary class relations of eighteenth-century Europe. Those born into wealthier families disdained their poorer neighbors and felt no compulsion to disguise their aversion. Many also assumed the inherent laziness of the poor, who, it was argued, never tried to get ahead, but would only work when starvation threatened.[5] Class-bound attitudes remain with us, of course; one twentieth-century southern historian of indentured servants adopted the attitude of the planters. "The servants were for the most part men and women of low grade, lazy, unambitious, ignorant, prone to small crimes and petty evasions."[6] The opinion of the Trustees, "those who are useless in London have proven to be useless in Georgia," echoes in the pages of historians of Georgia, perhaps excusing planters' turn to slavery.[7] In the eyes of the higher-ups, little separated the servants from the charity cases: heads of household were granted land and tools by the Trustees, who also guaranteed enough food until the first harvest. The poor might be divided into those considered worthy of philanthropy and those not, but those charity cases who did not succeed in transforming themselves from trades-men to farmers cannot be distinguished from servants in the derisive letters of the gentlemen. One early observer in Savannah described his poorer companions as "the idle and abandoned part of mankind . . . when they feel the many hardships and difficultys . . . they return like a dog to his vomite, to gratify those vicious habits of idleness and drinking." (This observer would later approach the Trustees for a handout.)[8] As these in-dividuals constitute the ancestors of many Americans, perhaps we might examine their experiences for ourselves.

The original shipload disembarked on February 1, 1733, and lived in tents for several months. Under Oglethorpe's close watch, the clearing for and construction of Savannah proceeded at first chaotically, until the workforce was divided into groups of carpenters and shingle makers who were taught to fell trees by enslaved African sawyers, whose labor was do-nated by South Carolinian gentlemen. Every fourth night, men served guard duty, heading straight back to construction work in the mornings. Little time or energy remained for farming their individual lots. A clear message about discipline and social order came in the form of a whipping sentence passed on a servant girl, "accused of a loose disorderly behav-iour"; two days later, as the girl was brought out by four armed men and a slave prepared to begin the lashing, Oglethorpe played the part of the benevolent patron. Sparing her the whip at the last moment, she was de-ported back to England instead.[9]

As spring turned to summer, the English succumbed to undiagnosed illnesses or "fevers" and began to die. By September, approximately forty new colonists were dead. About a quarter of the six hundred who had moved to Georgia by early 1734 would not survive the first year, leaving their mourning families bereft.[10] Even a quick glance at the Trustees' list of the settlers yields a sense of the grim atmosphere for many of those who had come with big dreams. William Calvert was a widower by July 4; Richard Cannon by July 22, having already lost a son in the Atlantic crossing; and James Carwell by September 7. Judith Clarke had lost her husband and two sons to the Georgia adventure by April 1734. So far from home, all normality gone, we can only imagine the trauma visited on these individuals. At first, Oglethorpe had awarded a solemn military funeral to the deceased, with guns firing and bells tolling, until "the people begane to die so fast that the frequent firing of the canon, and owr small arms, struck such terrour, in owr sick people (who knowing the cause, concluded they should be the next)." Oglethorpe discontinued the practice.[11]

Records of the ill describe "bloody Fluxes attended by Convulsions and other terrible Symptoms" or fevers leading to "a great trembling, after which great pain in my head and burning heat succeeded . . . this Fit had left me very much disorder'd."[12] High temperatures and the accompanying pain laid victims up for days, with little relief to be had in those days before convenient painkilling medications.[13] Many of these symptoms correspond to malaria and dysentery—high fevers and general aches—which were particularly dangerous for children. Oglethorpe, however, was convinced responsibility for all the sickness lay with rum consumption. Convinced that the new settlers were drinking themselves to death, he forbade any spirits immediately and strove to ensure that none circulated. The Trustees successfully lobbied the House of Commons to pass a law banning all liquor, but the colonists worked just as hard to secure access to it, seeking solace from the agonies of whatever other maladies their exposure to new microbes brought, let alone normal aches and pains such as "a violent Disorder in my Face occasioned by the Tooth-Ach."[14]

Illness haunted the colony for years and eighteenth-century medicine reads like a medieval sadist's party. Observers pondered the relief brought on by "some large Boils Breaking, which helped to discharge the Morbi-fick Matter," but mostly hoped for "the benefit of nature by plentifull Evacuation." Relying usually on bloodletting and vomiting to purge the body of any contaminants, the settlers of Georgia also tried rather more original solutions for ailments beyond the regular fevers and fluxes. A withered arm was treated with "a strap of human skin . . . tied around his very thin arm." The cure brought "marked improvement," not only to the arm but also to "holes on his chest and shoulders." Snake venom led to "the patient naked and buried practically up to his neck. A cobbler had given this advice."[15] Peter Gordon, the rather haughty first bailiff, struggling with the repellent-sounding "fistula in ano," sought relief in Charles Town, where he "was cutt three times and underwent incredible torture," eventually convincing Oglethorpe of his need to return to England.[16]

The most common treatment for any and all diagnoses, bloodletting, would be performed by a "barber-surgeon." In the early eighteenth century, someone referred to as a barber was as likely as a surgeon to drain blood, lance a boil, or set a bone. Bloodletting might prove rather unpleasant, if one already suffered from a raging fever. Citing a medical book, a pastor recommended those enduring fever "should have one's blood let often and mix saltpeter or spirits of vitriol in one's drinking water." Explaining one resistant patient's ordeal, he reported, "they tapped a vein in his head and, because the blood would not run, after that a vein in his arm . . . We had several men at hand who were holding him."[17] No current research supports bloodletting for high temperatures, but it seemed to have offered a placebo effect to some, one recipient testifying to "immediate Ease" afterward.[18] The only effective treatment for the many fevers brought on by the malaria-carrying *Anopheles* mosquito was quinine, derived from the bark of the cinchona tree of South America. Jesuit missionaries had passed on this cure to other European powers, but the limited availability of "Jesuits Bark," as most called it, made it very expensive.[19]

Oglethorpe blamed rum for both the illness and the rebellious behavior. Yet it should not surprise us that, surviving under that primitive level of medical knowledge, so many determined that pain-numbing alcohol was an absolute necessity to get through the daily grind. Despite the elite's complaints about drunkenness as the scourge of the working classes, nothing particularly excessive characterized the level of rum consumption in 1730s Georgia. Booze flowed freely in the taverns of their neighbors to the north, too. Alcohol consumption in 1770s New York, where a tavern for every thirteen adult white men tempted the workforce, averaged around 10 ounces of spirits daily, while the sober Bostonians of Puritan background sipped a mere seven shots each day.[20] Given the foreignness of the colonial experience to the newly arrived Georgians, and the numbers of people dying around them, we might be surprised if they did not seek a little escape from their despair. Little compassion emanated from their masters. British class distinctions dehumanized servants, and these notions were certainly carried to Georgia where masters wasted no emotions on their subordinates. "One dyed . . . of ye Scurveys and a Dropsie. Ye other about 3 weeks ago of a Dropsie and an ulcer in his leg . . . Ye death of them 2 is a £100 loss to me."[21]

Meanwhile, Oglethorpe traveled back and forth to Charles Town, purchasing supplies and discussing matters of security. Focusing on defense against the Spanish and potentially hostile Indians, he also directed the establishment of forts along the coast and the interior. Fort Argyle, after a first site proved unsuitable, was completed west of Savannah in the early fall and manned by rangers. Fort Thunderbolt was designed to protect the Wilmington River access to the town, whereas a lighthouse and small fort at Tybee Island should guard the Savannah River. Skidaway Island, also to the southeast of Savannah, seemed like a perfect place to put a defense against the Spanish. About ten households set up home at each of these locales. Farming was impossible, given the soils; those who made any progress became Indian traders, only to have that activity banned by Oglethorpe, who tried to maintain strict controls of the trade. The isolation, crop failures, and frustrations with maintaining buildings led to gradual abandonment. None would prove successful; only Argyle remained by 1740.[22]

In 1736, Oglethorpe told surveyor Noble Jones to lay out a town and fort up-country at the head of the Savannah, to be named Augusta. (Frederick, the prince of Wales, had just married Princess Augusta of Saxe-Gotha. The fort at the southernmost point in the colony would be named Frederica.) Already some "warehouses" stood, built by frontier traders who ventured out beyond the effective reach of colonial governors. After some false starts, local Chickasaws disenchanted with South Carolina pledged their help and the fort was serviceable by the spring of 1738. Although Oglethorpe appointed a military command, he saw the spot as "Key of all the Indian Countrey," a way to divert the lucrative Indian trade profits from Charles Town to Georgia. This move would spark fury from the Carolinians, especially as Oglethorpe ordered the seizure and destruction of all trade goods and rum held by anyone without a Georgia license to trade, a command carried out with some gusto by Oglethorpe's deputy to the area, Roger Lacy. (Lacy's temper might have been occasioned by his "drinking too liberally.") Despite a long legal dispute with the South Carolinians, the region, mostly peopled by Indians who had previously traded with South Carolina merchants, would grow to become a thriving deerskin business hub and remain largely outside the sphere of influence of Savannah's officials. By 1739, a road was under construction to connect the trading post to the coast, for boats struggled against the current to reach the northern town.[23]

■ In Savannah, now surrounded by sickness and death, some rather desperate workers thought they should take over the management of their own affairs.[24] The efforts of the "better sort" were less than impressive, after all. As an English gentleman described it, "an intended rising of the meaner Sort of Inhabitants" stirred when, in Oglethorpe's absence, his second-in-command, Captain Scott, ordered Samuel Gray to send his servant "to attend him and the rest of the gentlemen that came to visit the colony." Gray protested and built up support from "the common people with whome he conversed," giving the bailiffs considerable trouble. They finally managed to deliver the servant to the authorities, but for his dissension, Gray was placed in the stocks and Oglethorpe encouraged him to leave in June.[25] No onlooker could have failed to understand that British class status and power relations should supposedly transfer even to the colonial wilderness.

As the summer of 1733 progressed, the Londoners tried to adjust to the southern heat and humidity, the likes of which they had never felt. They managed to construct twenty-one houses, despite the deaths of five carpenters in one July week. While the first settlers suffered, the Trustees busied themselves organizing more shipments of people; 183, some "reduced to the last extremity of want," departed in October. At the end of the year, they also granted 500 acres each to a group of Scottish Lowlanders who intended to bring servants with them when they emigrated the following summer. These individuals embraced a vision of America in keeping with their cultural norms: southern Scottish gentry dominated their peasants much as Russian nobles did their serfs.[26] Just as they applied for these grants, their equivalents on the American mainland, South Carolinian planters, were trying to bribe Oglethorpe into arranging grants of large tracts of land and permitting them to bring their slaves south that first summer. Such offers highly offended Oglethorpe; "had it not been necessary to carry things with great temper here I should have kicked the proposers," he reported to the Trustees.[27]

Silk, not slave-tended rice, was supposed to become the cash crop of Georgia. The efforts of the Italian Amatis brothers to get the planting under way in the Public Garden ranked near the top of the colony's priorities. Paul Amatis, his expertise in silk allowing him to negotiate better terms from the Trustees than almost anyone, began his work in Charles Town, starting the mulberry nursery on which such high hopes lay. He would not bring the saplings to Savannah until the fall of 1734.[28] The rest of the settlers tried to suddenly become farmers on their fifty-acre country lots and builders on their town lots, and they experienced great difficulties achieving either. Many of the city lots, assigned before examination of the ground, did not lend themselves to their purpose. Egmont designated them in retrospect as "lot: swamp overflow'd," a descriptor that can give only a small sense of the aggravation the families endured.

Farming proved impossible for many. The timber that had to be cleared, the plowing and planting of poor soils with musty seeds, the fencing to protect the crops from the free range livestock, never mind the wildlife, all to be done while sick or in mourning; nothing of the situation bred success. The observant would notice that even the most sober and industrious met with little happiness in the first year.[29] The Public Stores annual allotment of fifteen bushels of corn, a barrel of meat, and sixteen gallons of molasses kept the colony going, but depended upon the storekeeper's ability to procure such provisions. By the second summer, the Trustees believed households should be providing for themselves and assumed those who requested an extension of rations needed to be investigated for idleness.[30]

However, toward the end of 1733, a buoyant Oglethorpe looked with pride on his achievement. By all accounts "indefatigable" in his efforts, he had launched a total of nine settlements, populated by 437 surviving individuals. Fifty homes stood complete in Savannah with many more under way; civil government ran to his liking; a mill, a forge, and a lighthouse at Tybee were under construction; the settlers continued to clear their lots for a spring planting; local Indians remained friends; and a militia drilled under a defined command structure. (See Fig. 1.) When a sloop filled with starving Irish convicts sentenced to Jamaican servitude appeared in the harbor after being refused landing, he took the initiative and purchased them without authorization from London. Dispensed around the colony to serve widows, the magistrates, the Public Garden, and other Trust lands, the Irish seemed a bargain—hundreds of man-years of labor for only 200 pounds.[31] Oglethorpe readied to depart for England, satisfied with his endeavors. The Salzburgers delayed him; they arrived in March, and he spent time assisting their settlement in Ebenezer, finally setting sail in early May with a delegation of Creeks, including Tomochichi.

He brought a Planter to treat with him, as it were for the
Purchase of these two Servants, my Husband and me, and there
we were formally sold to him.[32]
—Defoe, *Moll Flanders*

The Irish themselves seemed less thrilled with the deal. Sentenced to a life of servitude far from home and family, disdained by their British masters, they had nothing to gain from obedience. Culturally inclined to re-

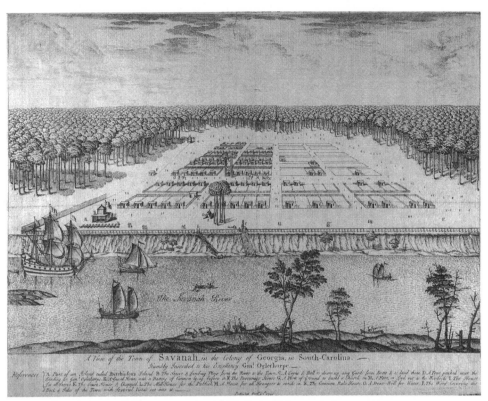

FIGURE 1. *Peter Gordon, "A View of Savannah," 1734. Courtesy of Hargrett Rare Book and Manuscript Library, University of Georgia Libraries.*

sist English authority, they refused to abide by the terms their class, ethnicity, and religion ascribed to them. "Vile rogues," Egmont called them, and undoubtedly they had been convicted of crimes. But in the eighteenth century, theft rose as prices increased; morality was a luxury often only the rich could afford. As Moll explains, "the wise Man's Prayer, *Give me not Poverty lest I Steal.* Let 'em remember that a time of Distress is a time of dreadful Temptation, and all the Strength to resist is taken away; Poverty presses, the Soul is made Desperate."[33] In any case, the new arrivals quickly earned a collective reputation as rather a bad influence.[34]

As Georgia approached its first anniversary, increasingly servants refused to cooperate. Magistrates doled out severe punishments in a futile attempt to bring a restless Savannah society under control. One woman sat in the stocks in the rain for three hours, followed by a trip into the harbor where she was ducked into the water. "In Ducking Her they Bruis'd her so against the Vessell she was lame for 2 or 3 Months after."[35] The Irish

Transports, labeled as ringleaders, certainly showed no respect to the masters assigned them. Mary Ochy's behavior was so "wicked & vile" that her master "could not endure her" in his home and promptly sold her.[36] Lost or burnt records leave us with only scattered remnants of court proceedings noted by Egmont, but these indicate a justice system designed to impose the traditional English class and ethnic order with the poor Irish at the very bottom. The harshest punishments were reserved for these Catholics, subjected to up to 100 lashes while their fellow drunken brawlers from England tended to receive fines.[37] Any servant caught trying to escape felt the sting of the lash, however.[38]

The death of William Wise in March 1734 led to the most serious charge, murder. Wise himself had been a troublemaker; among other things, he brought a prostitute on board his ship to Georgia, claiming her as his daughter.[39] Oglethorpe designated Wise overseer of several Trust servants on Hutchinson's Island, including a couple of the Irish, Alice Riley and Richard White. Judging by his sexual proclivities, Wise probably raped Riley. She gave birth to a son nine months after Wise's death. One morning, presumably the day after Wise had assaulted her, the two Irish servants brought water and a comb to his bedside, as he insisted they wash his long hair. According to the magistrate's account, while White choked him with a handkerchief, Riley dipped his head into the pail, effectively strangling and drowning him simultaneously.[40] Most of the colony assumed the motive was theft. But the servants could not have disposed of his goods, nor could they gain their freedom merely because Wise was dead; their indenture would have been passed on to another settler. They had nowhere to run. This lack of options points only to a crime of passion, and the timeline of the pregnancy suggests Riley asked White to help her kill him in response to Wise's rape.

White and Riley were arrested, and she confessed. Sentenced in May to execution, at some point they managed to escape into the woods, attempting to forage for survival. Spotted by some settlers, White was apprehended and marched, held by his neck, into town, where despite his protestations of innocence, the colonists led him "immediately to the Gallows." Riley was recaptured soon afterwards. Now visibly pregnant, she was allowed to deliver her son on December 21 and nurse him for a month before her hanging, all the time claiming she had wrongfully confessed. The baby, named James, died a month after his mother. Their Catholicism was duly noted by their captors.[41]

The colonists were gripped again by illness during the early summer of 1734, and morale spiraled downward around Savannah. New ideas emerged both to explain the fevers plaguing the colony and to find potential cures. Several people suspected the available food was the source. "Tis impossible to keep meat from being tainted here in Summer Time," complained one who had feared for his life; another was convinced that "Eating so much Salt Meat Heats the Blood & causes the Scurvy." Contrary to the gentlemen's notion that liquor created the problem, some believed that rum spared them from sickness. By the following winter, this notion had spread throughout the community.[42]

Presiding over the colony in the dual role of magistrate and keeper of the Public Stores, Thomas Causton wielded extraordinary power after Oglethorpe's departure. A calico printer by trade, Causton's correspondence reveals an intelligent and literate man, yet not a man whose birth garnered him genteel status or obedience in England. Limited contact with the Trustees, given the distance and infrequency of ships in Savannah, meant he determined the fate of many colonists. Although the consensus regarded him "the most Capable of Such an Office," when things went wrong, "all the Reproaches Seems to be Levelled at him." His harsh punishments issued from the bench (necessary, he felt, to keep order on the frontier) coupled with unpopular decisions about who was and who was not entitled to free rations provoked opposition during the fall of 1734. Causton played in a no-win scenario. Although the Trustees thought him a spendthrift, handing out too much food to idle settlers, some Georgians begged for help and denounced him as "our Imperious Magistrate" if he cut them off.[43]

To decipher whether Causton was fair or corrupted by his power demands we pay very close attention to those condemning him. Criticism emanated chiefly from the wealthier sort, who had paid their own way to Georgia, taken 500 acres of freehold land grants and brought servants. Answering to a lower-ranked man rankled their egos. Some refused to cooperate or to fulfill jury or militia duty, "Saying they are Gentlemen and it is beneath them to Serve in an Inferiour Court."[44]

One of these freeholders, a hothead named Joseph Watson, entered into a partnership at a local trading post occupied by Mary and John Musgrove, whose presence in the region preceded the Georgia Charter. The daughter of an Indian woman and a deerskin trader, Mary Musgrove operated the local trading post with a succession of husbands. The Musgroves had welcomed the new colony (although they counted themselves not subject to the rules of the Trustees and owned at least one slave) and guided Oglethorpe into smooth relations with local Indians. When Oglethorpe brought Tomochichi and a delegation of Indians to England in May 1734,

John Musgrove traveled too, as interpreter for the trip. During the fall of 1734, Watson worked in his place, drinking a lot with Indians trading at the post and bragging in town that he had caused the alcoholic poisoning death in September of one of the Indian businessmen known as Captain Skee. Watson gradually soured all the Indians who regularly traded at Musgroves when he attacked and beat another, Eusteeche, in a dispute about prices and they all refused to bring deerskins any longer. Dreading the more violent consequences of an Indian reprisal on the colony, Causton pleaded with Eusteeche to allow the colony to charge Watson with wrongdoing rather than to seek vengeance himself. Watson was fined, and Causton cautioned him in court to negotiate honestly in the future. But more detailed investigation uncovered that Watson not only defrauded Indians but also the Musgroves. Ordered to vacate the Musgroves' premises in early November, Watson instead locked himself inside. When Eusteeche and some companions arrived some days later with skins to trade and discovered Watson was locked inside, they broke in. Watson escaped but in the ensuing chaos, Eusteeche killed Justice, an enslaved man owned by the Musgroves.[45]

Causton and the other magistrates found themselves with a diplomatic problem. With Tomochichi out of the country, they brokered a compromise. They had promised Eusteeche and the Indians that they would not have to do business with Watson again and understood Eusteeche's anger at finding Watson in control of the post. No one would seek justice for the ironically named slave, although the Musgroves would demand compensation. But to keep peace, the magistrates encouraged Eusteeche to stay out of Savannah. They warned Watson that his life was in danger and advised him to leave town.

Watson, however, continued to drink heavily and boast publically about the death of Skee. Still fearing an Indian war, Causton charged him with misdemeanors and instructed the jury to find him guilty, but "Lunatick," allowing Causton to keep him confined in Savannah. It was into this situation that the ship from England carrying Tomochichi and John Musgrove sailed shortly after Christmas. To exacerbate matters, Peter Gordon, still the official first bailiff, accompanied them. Destined to stay in Savannah for only two months, Gordon fancied himself Causton's social better and refused to work with him. Instead he spent time socializing and sympathizing with the disgruntled freeholders, calling into question Causton's reordering of the racial hierarchy between English and Indian.[46]

Given his official position, Gordon could have overturned the decision, but he had no designs to stay in Georgia. Declaring "it was not very gentle usage to Imprison a Man for the sake of an Indian," he indulged the conniving behavior of the disgruntled freeholders and offered to represent them in London. In Charles Town by March 1 and awaiting passage, Gordon received a packet of letters from his Savannah friends. Another drama was unfolding in town, and Causton was in the thick of it.[47]

The people of Savannah were suddenly alerted by alarm bells on the evening of the first Sunday in March 1735. A young girl had told her boss that one of the Irish servants had been conspiring with others to instigate an insurrection, slaughtering their masters and burning the town. Those involved tied a red string around their wrist as a silent signal to others of their complicity. In the absence of the magistrates, a local man mustered the freeholders and sent out search parties to check on the servants in every home. Three men found wearing strings were apprehended, one of them an Irish transport. An Irishwoman and a younger boy were caught later. A gulf opened immediately between rumor and reality around the Red String Plot. Stories flew rampantly that the Irish readied to loose their murderous wrath on the colonists; perhaps the Indians also. A full guard stood by all night, cannons poised against any assault.[48]

Causton returned from a visit to Thunderbolt some hours later. He immediately assumed Watson and his ally Parker fermented the trouble, imagining they had hired some "Villainous fellows" to cause havoc and then would blame Musgrove and his Indian friends. This groundless theory led Causton to order searches of the homes of Parker and Watson, where nothing incriminating was found. It became clear fairly quickly that neither Musgrove nor any Indians were implicated at all. The five servants, speedily found guilty of treason despite their protests of innocence, received sixty lashes. The matter confirmed, as far as most freeholders were concerned, that the servants of Georgia, especially the Irish, were the worst sort of despicable scum.[49]

In fact, Causton discovered before the end of the month that the Irish had not been organizing any rebellion. The entirety of the Red String Plot was a "Drunken Resolution" by a few free English colonists who, finding themselves deeply in debt, swore one night they would abandon Savannah. But Causton decided privately that it was in the best interests of the colony not to make this public. The horrendous whipping of the servants would serve as a deterrent to the actual ringleaders going forward. The magistrate felt it wise to let some calm return to the settlement.[50]

Through the spring of 1735, Causton's control of law and order continued to disintegrate, however, and he complained to the Trustees that there could be no preventing access to rum. Finding a jury willing to convict their peers proved almost impossible, whether charged with selling liquor or killing the Trustees' cattle. Oglethorpe received disparaging reports of disobedient servants, apparently encouraged by others at an illegal tavern run by Mrs. Penrose, one of the first arrivals and sarcastically referred to as "Conqueror Over the whole place." Even the constables refused to cooperate, arguing with Causton and releasing prisoners at their own whim. One master requested "4 pair hand Cuffs." "I find a great many Saucey Villians in this Country that don't incline to Submitt to any Government, and there is an absolute Necessity to make Examples of some for the Terror of others."[51] Those made an example of tended to be Irish; Isaac Fling and John Fox endured 100 and 60 lashes respectively for stealing in May. Even one sympathetic to Causton observed that the punishments were "too Severe."[52]

Servitude and hard Labour were things Gentlemen
could never stoop to.
—Defoe, *Moll Flanders*

The rough equality stemming from frontier conditions eroded class distinctions, including the fine divisions between the higher ranks. In December 1734, Sir Francis Bathurst brought his family to Georgia to restore their fortune. He arranged to stay temporarily with Walter Augustin, master of four servants, who had moved from South Carolina and lived six miles upriver from Savannah. Bathurst's expectations of appropriate deference from the provincial were disappointed. "He kept me and my family worse than ever I kept my Dogs in England, upon my complaint to his wife and him about it he threatened to beat my Teeth down my Throat, and to send me to the Logg house at Savanna *and told me I was not in England but in America.*" Augustin's version of events did not dispute Bathurst, but reflected how he saw it: "None of my Bisness to Serve Him but as he thought fit."[53]

The first of another set of gentlemen, the Lowland Scots, had begun to establish plantations on Sterlings Bluff, thirty miles south of Savannah. Wealthy by Georgia standards, they had been granted 500-acre lots that came with the promise of "all the Rights and Priviledges of a Gentleman. Among which Priviledges, One is, always to serve on horseback." Other rights accorded only the rich included hunting and fishing. To protect them from the poor, at least four gentlemen must serve as jurors in any court case against them.[54] Unsatisfied, the gentlemen now demanded that the

Trustees also provide them a year of sustenance and the tools and other supplies granted the charity cases. Causton understood the Trustees intended nothing of the sort and refused.[55]

Meanwhile servants and the poor around the colony upset etiquette further by hunting and fishing to feed themselves, thereby robbing their betters of the pleasures of exclusive, status-earning behaviors.[56] Some had become skillful hunters from necessity. "Being Christmas Eve, my People desired Leave to go out this morning to provide themselves a Dinner tho we have good Beeff Porke Cheese Flower &c. They are now come home and have brought 3 ½ Coople of Ducks, 1 paire of Doves one Turkey and a fine Buck," reported one grandee, torn between relief that he was not out of pocket and surprise at the very association of servants and hunting, the marker of a gentleman.[57] Although hunting had seemed outside their cultural possibilities in England, especially after the Black Act, target practice for the poor had been provided by the philanthropists. Much of the livestock provided to the colony by the Trustees escaped. "We had some Hogs but they are run wild and left us." "The Cows and Calves which we had are all run into the woods." Upon these chattels the laborers learned to shoot and to butcher. "Felons, Runaway servants etc have molested the Inland Parts of the Country and thieving . . . is grown so common that great numbers of Hogs and not a few Cattel, have been killed in the Woods." The consequences of stealing from the Trustees illustrate the difficulties of the better sort in policing early Georgia. Juries acquitted their peers on any charges of poaching, for like the Blacks of Waltham, the people had not yet surrendered their ownership of the forests.[58]

Beyond that, those charity householders whose farming efforts failed to produce enough offered their labor for sale to the gentlemen, but at such high rates as offended their potential employers. Servants and tradesmen found their labor to be of much greater value than in London. As one mill owner complained, "The charge of white Laborers being so extravigently Deare there is no such thing as bearing it." Another pleaded with the Trustees to send more servants as he found "Carpenters Labor is very Dear." "I cannot afford to pay Journeymen," cried another early settler. One observed, "If a thing requires a lot of work, the locksmiths and blacksmiths make one pay dearly for it."[59] Ordinary Georgians left us few words, but the frustrations of those hoping to exploit them speak volumes.

So the disenchantment spread. As the lower orders realized they must fend for themselves, respect for masters gradually dissolved. The lack of respect drove the gentlemen to anger. Causton, as representative of the

Trustees, stood in the middle, taking flak from both, trying to put the colony on the footing his bosses expected. The breach of the societal hierarchy provoked the better sort into protests of a different nature. They began to clamor for the introduction of slavery, to rid themselves of this insolent servant class. In late May 1735, Patrick Tailfer and the other Scottish gentry took up their quills to make their case.

This initial plea from the group who would become known as the Malcontents bore little of the vituperative sarcasm that would characterize later statements. They instead made a case against the use of British servants. The climate sickened white workers, so they were "useless for almost one half of the Year," claimed Tailfer. Then followed an outline of the costs of maintaining the workforce. British workers must be "cloathed as Europeans," whereas slaves could be given much less. Apparently, Africans remained in good health on a cheaper diet, never mind the outlay on beer and liquor that the British servants needed, "otherwise they turn feeble and languid and are not capable to perform their Work." A strange argument indeed, that alcohol was fuel for English servants and not their ruin. In any case, the British servants would have to be replaced after their terms, which apparently involved either expensive travel back to the homeland to find suitable candidates or the acceptance of transported criminals. At this point, the protests grew into a vehement screed against the Catholic Irish of Georgia, "Skill'd in all manner of Villainy," blaming them for the "Plots and treasonable Designs" that shook the colony a few weeks before.

Now skin color entered the argument, for as the Scots explained, runaway servants could easily escape. "There is no Law as yet made to take up white People who are travelling," whereas "Negroes would always be known" as slaves and anyone might ask them for a pass. As a compromise with the Trustees' goal of producing poor and hardworking Englishmen, the would-be planters promised they would never use slaves in skilled trades, only for hard labor, felling trees, and beating rice. The Trustees could limit the number to a safe ratio, if they pleased.

The letter concluded with a reminder of another dreadful inconvenience of employing servants after their indenture, "namely their Wages." Feeding, clothing, and paying people for their work surely required too heavy of a burden for these men to bear. In their eyes, and they presumed, the eyes of all their fellow English gentlemen, ownership of slaves was essential.[60] The letter brought only scorn from Egmont.

At this point, the Malcontents made no mention of another grievance stirring among the colonists: the conditions of land tenure. The Trustees had imposed "tail-male" tenure, which meant that only males could inherit land. But given the death rates in the colony, many felt this policy unreasonable as it might leave wives and daughters destitute; thus they sent requests back to London that the philanthropists reconsider. At a meeting that summer, however, the Trustees refused, worrying that daughters might marry men from other colonies and desert Georgia. "If such daughters marry persons approved of by us who will settle on the fathers grant," they would give the land to her husband. This translated into the Trustees appointing themselves guardians for even adult women, having veto power over their choice of spouse.[61] In any case, small farmers felt insecure about their holdings and over the next few years, the Malcontents would exploit this concern, presenting themselves to their neighbors as men with similar issues. In petitions to the Trustees, they would bring up the tenure grumblings, wrapping them up with their demands for slavery into a package of complaints.

One grievance the Trustees could address. In a fortunate coincidence, another letter from Georgia disparaging the minister, Rev. Quincy, as neglectful of his duties, arrived just at the moment the Trustees heard that two pious young gentlemen from Oxford University by the name of Wesley volunteered to convert the Indians of Georgia to Christianity. In October 1735, the Trustees fired Quincy and replaced him with John Wesley. Wesley and his brother Charles prepared to sail with Oglethorpe in the fall. Embarking in October, the Wesleys would join a contingent of new settlers, including a group of Moravians, other Pietists from Salzburg, Germany, and almost 200 Scottish Highlanders. Delays meant they did not set sail until December, rather disheartening for the frugal Egmont, for it meant they would arrive too late in the year to plant, "whereby we Shall have two years provision to furnish the Passengers instead of One." Money, however, was not all he should have worried about.[62]

3

DISCONTENT, 1736–1739

It is easier for a camel to go through the eye of a needle than
for a rich man to enter into the Kingdom of God.
—Matthew 19:24

On death row in the horrific dungeons of Newgate Gaol, the wily prostitute-thief Moll Flanders luckily—quite suddenly—found the Lord and thereby secured a remission of her capital sentence. She described the Gospels as "a Scheme of infinite Mercy, proclaim'd from Heaven to Sinners of the greatest Magnitude." Moll always loved a scheme.[1] Instead of death, the court banished her to the American colonies, where she quickly became a wealthy woman and lived happily ever after. She rarely mentioned God again. No one can ever know the sincerity or depth of another's religious faith, but the authenticity of Moll's conversion and religious devotion might well be questioned. Her honesty remained far from complete. Survivors struggling at the bottom of a society must do what they can to get by.

Daniel Defoe published *Moll Flanders* in 1722, shortly before Georgia founder James Oglethorpe investigated England's jails and came up with the idea of giving the imprisoned a fresh start in the American South. Defoe, however, was a leading dissenter. Although English authorities saw pulpits as instruments of social control, dissenters found a different message in the Gospel: an early liberation theology that elevated the poor in God's eyes, turning the world upside down. Defoe had defended the religious freedom of Quakers in the South Carolina colony. He viewed the American South as a haven, where those who championed equality before God might escape both poverty and the controls of an Anglican church that supported social hierarchies.[2]

The story of the Great Awakening of the late 1730s and early 1740s is usually confined to New England and the mid-Atlantic colonies.[3] However, the leading figures of that Atlantic phenomenon, John Wesley and George Whitefield, who were considered two of the most dangerous men in the British Empire, served as Savannah's first ministers. Wesley arrived in town just as the Malcontents festered discontent. Still early in the process of formulating his theology, Wesley's time in Georgia fostered disobedience against the colonial magistrates. Whitefield followed him and loudly condoned his rejection of the clerical authority of the established Church. Although Whitefield and Wesley did not need to raise the consciousness of the poor about their exploitation, they do seem to have regenerated a population unmoored from its home culture and provided a sanction for action. Between them, these men unintentionally encouraged what we have come to call the death of deference, inherent in the Christian gospels. In a place without any of Walpole's oppressive infrastructure, where social order already teetered, the theology of the lowly Christ seriously threatened the Malcontents' dream of positioning themselves as a planter elite.

E. P. Thompson unveiled the "slumbering Radicalism" in dissenting churches between the 1660 Restoration and 1790s England. He criticized Wesley's Methodism for crushing the rebellious spirit set free by Thomas Paine, by encouraging quiet reflection instead of public action.[4] But the Methodism of the late eighteenth century cannot be equated with the primitive church Wesley sought to emulate in 1730s Georgia: a church he believed he witnessed firsthand in the Moravians who traveled to America with him in late 1735 and with whom he stayed for his first formative weeks in the colony.[5] Inspired by their humility and their fearlessness in the face of danger, Wesley, and later Whitefield, preached a message that threatened the Georgian order.

Charles Wesley had founded a "Holy Club" at Oxford University in the late 1720s, and John quickly took a leadership role. Despising the corrupt patronage system of the Anglican Church, the brothers wanted to restore a simple and true devotion to Christ in themselves and others; as one biographer describes, they had a "passion for piety." Another resident of the Oxford community, George Whitefield, joined the group. Whitefield worked as a 'servitor' at the university, a poor student who served others in return for tuition waivers. Although the members of the Holy Club held to the theology of salvation by faith, they believed strongly in the model of the lowly Christ who had lived among the poor. They visited jails and workhouses regularly, reaching out to the real "Molls" and attempting to emulate the primitive church. The death of one of their club after such visits drew attention and some derision to the group, often called the Oxford Methodists, although they remained within the Church of England establishment. "They read prayers every day in the common gaol, preach every Sunday and administer the sacraments once a month. They almost starve themselves to be able to relieve the poor and buy books for their conversion. They attempt to reform notorious whores." That this description was meant as a severe criticism of religious extremists allows some insight into the normally low expectations of an eighteenth-century Anglican churchman.[6]

James Oglethorpe had reached out to friends at Oxford, hoping to locate pastors for the Georgia settlers and missionaries for the Indians. The Wesley brothers responded with enthusiasm because the project seemed to offer them a chance to test the purity of their faith and, like St. Paul, bring Christianity to pagans who would surely embrace the message of redemption they carried. Along with Holy Club companions Benjamin Ingham and Charles Delamotte, the brothers set sail for Georgia in December 1735.

The long, tough journey across the Atlantic proved pivotal in the early development of Wesley's theology. A storm came close to destroying their vessel, but a group of Moravians on board remained calm, singing hymns together throughout the trauma. Wesley, fascinated by their serenity, joined their evening services, hoping to achieve their deep level of faith. He compared the Moravians to the early church, whose simple living demonstrated a rejection of worldly values, including the pursuit of status. The imitation of Christ required the devotee to pursue humility, in the manner of Christ's washing of the feet of the apostles. Observing how the Moravians on board had been "performing those servile offices for the other passengers, which none of the English would undertake," Wesley considered that their stoicism during the storm had come from a security in God's love stemming from the humble behaviors that brought them closer to Christ.[7]

After his arrival in Georgia in February 1736, he stayed with the Moravian community for a few weeks, and his preaching in Savannah was most influenced by their teachings. He began his role as pastor in March, replacing Rev. Quincy, who had at best attracted twenty people to his Sunday services; "religion," as Quincy complained, "seems to be the least minded of anything in the place."[8] Oglethorpe discouraged any missionary activity to the Indians, arguing that Savannah needed Wesley more than Georgia's native population. In this Oglethorpe was right; the Creeks showed little interest in religious conversion. Wesley's bitter evaluation of all the tribes of the region upon his departure, based upon the testimony of traders and other travelers, excused his failure to fulfill his missionary intentions. "They are likewise, all except (perhaps) the Choctaws, gluttons, drunkards, thieves, dissemblers, liars. They are implacable, unmerciful; murderers of fathers, murderers of mothers, murderers of their own children . . . Whoredom they account no crime."[9]

In Savannah, however, Wesley developed a following over the course of the year, calling it "O blessed place!" He expended more energy than his predecessor, making door-to-door visits of his parishioners, organizing a religious society among the most devout, and studying both German and Spanish in hopes of reaching diverse settlers, even a few Sephardic Jews. Delamotte's school taught the young to read and to write, and on Sundays he led a catechism class. Wesley's religious message included sometimes scathing critiques of the regular Anglican clergy. When added to his theological vision, "I was not . . . a respecter of persons; but was determined . . . to behave indifferently to all, rich or poor,"[10] as he recorded in his diary that summer, those critiques produced political repercussions, in ways he could not have predicted.

Several years later, the Malcontents argued that Wesley corrupted the poor during his stay in Georgia, arguing that he "tended to propagate a Spirit of Indolence, and of Hypocrisy among the most abandoned; it being much easier for such Persons, by an affected Shew of Religion, and Adherence to Mr. *Wesly*'s Novelties, to be provided by his Procurement from the publick Stores, than to use that Industry which *true* Religion recommends: Nor indeed could the Reverend Gentleman conceal the Designs he was so full of, having frequently declar'd, *That he never desir'd to see* Georgia *a Rich, but a Religious Colony.*"[11]

Neither Tailfer nor Wesley left us records of exactly how Wesley preached most Sundays in Savannah, but his attachment to the ethos of the primitive (pre-Constantine) church at this point in his religious development leaves clues as to how he may have influenced his parish. The image of Christ as a friend to the poor and the sick, "the most abandoned," counteracted the very essence of eighteenth-century gentry norms. Those at the top of society were not to be revered for they lived furthest from God, whatever mollification noblesse oblige brought to their conscience. Riches in Heaven were destined for those who had none on Earth.[12] The so-called Protestant work ethic played no part in Wesley's teaching.

Gradually Wesley built a following, including a young lady named Sophia Hopkey, niece of the Trustees' chief administrator in the colony, Thomas Causton. The unrequited feelings Wesley held for Hopkey would cause great consternation in the town. She married another suitor in the spring of 1737, and the young clergyman's heartache overwhelmed his good sense. That summer he publicly refused her communion and provoked a firestorm, unleashing political uproar as well as religious and personal dissension. Hopkey's new husband, supported by Causton, brought charges against Wesley, claiming he had slandered her reputation out of personal jealousies.

Yet Wesley received a lot of backing from the community. Members of the grand jury impaneled to hear his case defended him in a letter to the Trustees, claiming "the whole charge against Mr Wesley is an artifice of Mr Causton's."[13] Causton, as keeper of the stores, held the most important position of authority in Savannah during Oglethorpe's frequent absences. In obeying the Trustees' commands, he had alienated many colonists, and so his fight with Wesley over his niece galvanized opposition to political control in the fall of 1737. Wesley would not bow down to Causton's political authority. He retained strong opinions about the authority of clergy over their flock, and the congregation rallied around him, while the Malcontents, furious at Wesley's philosophy and leadership, now clustered behind Causton, as the lesser of two evils. They had their own complaints about his leadership, but "openly, on all Occasions, took part with the Magistrates, in Opposition to any Sedition."[14]

As a representative of the less powerful members of Savannah's society, Wesley's religious leadership now spilled over into the political arena. Records are not entirely clear, but open defiance of the magistrates followed in October. The magistrates accused Wesley of leading this protest, not of disgruntled servants, but of men who had been entrusted with responsibilities in the colony. "Mr. Wesley and he, and some others, who were closely link'd in opposing the Magistrates in the Execution of Justice, used to come into the Court in a menacing Manner, crying out, Liberty, calling to the People to remember they were *Englishmen* &c., and that Mr. Wesley was generally the principal Speaker to harangue the People, though he had no Sort of Business, or any call there."[15] Summed up in Trustee Egmont's notes as "Rioters in open court," Burton the carpenter, Salter the bricklayer, Burnside the teacher, and Coates the constable refused to defer and instead claimed the rights of Englishmen.[16]

■ A new Trustee official, William Stephens, stepped into this maelstrom just two weeks later. Appointed as the new secretary for the colony, the Trustees hoped that Stephens would communicate more often than either Oglethorpe or Causton had done in the first few years of settlement. Struggling to understand the situation, he reported to the Trustees that the matter "had now drawn almost the whole Town into Parties in the Quarrel."[17] As Stephens spent his initial weeks in the colony, he met with various groups trying to sway him to their side. Causton and the magistrates' complaints about the minister show that they wanted to exploit the situation to rid themselves of Wesley.

Although the Malcontents had been angered by the colonial administration of Causton and his fellow magistrates, now they had a common enemy. As a result of Wesley's reminding the settlers of their rights, the magistrates claimed they were accorded no deference. Stephens sympathized with them; he privately told the Trustees that one of the magistrates could not afford fine clothing; his outfit was "very little better than the common Sort of the Populace." Stephens agreed that this would lead to disrespect for the justice system, "which upon the Bench must appear despicable." Indeed, the magistrates had no legal training, and the residents knew it. But the Trustees regarded lawyers as rascals and had pointedly sent none. They wanted the people of Savannah to defer to the magistrates because of social status. A few years later, when one Georgia magistrate actually had some legal expertise, Oglethorpe encouraged him to move to Charles Town and sought to replace him with an "industrious young man who . . . is very honest and sober, and is no attorney."[18]

It might be thought that Causton and the Malcontents only spoke ill of Wesley's egalitarian philosophy as a result of the Hopkey affair, were it not for the corroboration Stephens offered in his journal entry a week later. That Sunday, Wesley chose the Gospel text about 'rendering onto Caesar' as his sermon topic, discussing "Christian Liberty" and the extent to which citizens should "insist on their Rights when they found themselves oppressed by inferior Magistrates exercising discretionary authority."[19] His defense of the powerless and bolstering of their sense of somebodiness before God carried over into the political and legal arenas. So the Malcontents needed to drive him away.

They succeeded. Wesley prepared to leave Georgia, believing he could not expect justice in the civil case against him. He escaped under cover of darkness, aided by several men. Stephens described one of them as "one of the principal Fomenters of Mischief . . . always taking upon him in Court to be an Advocate and Pleader for any Delinquent," and later revealed that four servants rowed Wesley to South Carolina. Accompanying him to England was Anne Charles, who had a record of "defamation," and James Campbell, disdainfully described by Egmont as an "idle fellow."[20] No one attempted to bring Wesley back for his trial. Even after his departure, in a continued effort to undermine any influence he might have exercised, Causton collected affidavits from some who claimed they knew that Wesley was a "Roman Priest" and that Campbell had had an illicit affair, with salacious details such as "the manner she put her legs and his manner of acting very obscenely."[21]

But if the Malcontents breathed a sigh of relief, thinking they had dispatched this dangerous radical from their midst, they must have been horrified to learn another of those Oxford Methodists would soon take his place. George Whitefield and Wesley passed each other in the English port of Deal on February 1, 1738, as Whitefield sailed to Georgia. Once the Trustees learned of the turmoil Wesley had instigated, they sent a quick note to Whitefield, en route in Gibraltar, appointing him deacon of Savannah and emphasizing their concern "that Sobriety and Industry, and a due Reverence to the Magistracy will be constantly recommended by You."[22]

■ While Wesley revitalized religion in Savannah, other bands of people began building new settlements around the colony. The first group of refugee Pietist Salzburgers had arrived in Georgia in March 1734 and been joined by others at the end of the year. A third shipment of people sailed in Wesley's convoy in early 1736. The first group had a preponderance of miners, known for their strong culture of autonomy, perhaps explaining why they chose to cross the Atlantic when so many of the Pietist refugees chose Prussia or other Protestant parts of eastern Europe. But miners and their wives also practiced small-scale farming, including husbandry of cattle, hogs, sheep, and horses.[23] Pastor Johann Bolzius led the community who sought to create a Godly society, and Bolzius felt it best they maintain some distance from the corrupting influences of Savannah. Oglethorpe selected a site some twenty-five miles away, and the pastor chose the name Ebenezer. The Salzburgers faced no less sickness and death than their English neighbors in these initial two years, with more than half the newborns dying in 1735. Infant mortality was very high everywhere in the eighteenth century, but for a small group so far from their larger home community, we can imagine the desolation felt magnified. Their dedication to farming was rewarded only with withered crops, for the infertile sandy soil of Ebenezer would produce nothing. At first they believed wolves preyed on their livestock, but in later years would realize that "people who have absconded from Savannah" hunted down "the two fat hogs that were lost from our town."[24]

In early 1736, the community insisted to Oglethorpe that they must move to avoid starvation and chose a site on Red Bluff. Despite continued enormous hardships including a bad summer of ill health, the Salzburgers, bolstered by a faith that emphasized passivity to God's will, set about building shelters and clearing, tilling, and planting. Their diligence, noted by all who visited, contrasted sharply with the scene around Savannah.[25]

Meanwhile Scottish Highlanders, whose ethos strongly contrasted with that of their Lowland neighbors, settled the southern outpost of Darien in early 1736. Recruited for their reputation as ferocious warriors, their purpose was to serve the colony as the first line of defense against the Spanish. They immediately constructed a guardhouse and a battery and proceeded to build forts on Cumberland and St. Simon's Islands, the latter known as Frederica. Attempts at farming corn netted the same results as other settlers, failed harvests and bitter frustration, but like the Salzburgers, the industriousness of the Darien community impressed all who paid them a visit. They began to concentrate on cattle-raising and timbering.[26]

The Highlanders, some of whom spoke only Scots Gaelic, had relatively little interaction with the people of Savannah and made no personal connections with the Lowlanders who composed the Malcontents. Wesley made two trips to the military community at Frederica that summer, and continued to try to pastor the soldiers there through the fall, but he found an unreceptive audience for his strict rules for a pious life. The community also stymied his companions in their attempts at ministry.[27]

Over the course of 1738, the disgruntled Lowlanders spent their time in the taverns around Savannah's sunny squares, endeavoring to build a coalition against the Trustees. Although most workers understood that slavery ran counter to their economic interests, the Malcontents listened to the grievances based on tail-male land tenure, a concern of many. Tail-male tenure meant that women could not inherit and Savannah's freeholders, having watched their neighbors die at a horrifying rate, wanted to protect their widows' and daughters' interests. As Tailfer and his friends considered their options, they gradually developed a strategy to blend the two very separate issues into one, "continually infusing into Peoples Heads bad notions of the Precariousness of their Tenure." As Stephens observed, in Malcontents' long diatribes to him, "a few Negroes was always at the end of it."[28] But they could not overcome the class differences. Some of the Malcontents kept illegal taverns, to which "many of the working people were drawn in, to spend what little money they had; or if they had none, they readily gave them Credit, and afterwards exacted Payment of them, by their Labour."[29] Kept in debt as a means to exploit them, working people felt no allegiance to the Malcontents. Whitefield's preaching would also undermine their attempts to build an alliance.

Whitefield was twenty-three years old and already a celebrity in England; soon he would be the most famous man in the British colonies. He joined the Holy Club at Oxford in 1733, attracted by their asceticism as a vehicle "to be meek, patient, and lowly" like Christ. When the Wesley brothers departed for America, he headed the Club, continuing the prison outreach. But Whitefield created a movement where the others had not. His charismatic preaching style broadened the appeal of the revival of religion, and soon participants attached the term "awakening" to the phenomenon that surrounded the young evangelist.[30]

Brewing around the Atlantic for two decades, what we now call the Great Awakening began as individual clerics in England, Scotland, Wales, and New England sought to revitalize their increasingly secularist societies through a conversion process that emphasized the Holy Spirit and a warm emotional relationship with God. Influenced tremendously by the German Pietist leader, Professor August Hermann Francke of the University of Halle, also the role model for the Salzburgers, these pastors understood that enthusiastic ministers were essential. The emotion they could generate in the audience would help those listening, first, to see their unworthiness, but then to attain the grace necessary for salvation. While Jonathan Edwards in Massachusetts and John Wesley in England generated followers, it was Whitefield's tours of Britain and later in the colonies that attracted the huge numbers of people enough to earn the Great Awakening a place in our history books.[31]

During Wesley's stint in Savannah, Whitefield became a star in England. Having experienced the joy of his own spiritual rebirth, he preached in a number of churches in London and then Bristol in 1737. Invited as a guest by ministers, Whitefield drew crowds with his theatrical performances and word spread rapidly about the new clergyman who could bring hundreds and soon thousands to tears and then joyous singing, as they confronted and atoned for their sins, were forgiven, and felt the warm glow of a rebirth in God's love. Although he looked up to Wesley, the public regarded Whitefield as the leader of the revival. His charm and energy contrasted with Wesley's austerity, and converted many who had come to church out of curiosity.

His startling success, however, also quickly provoked opposition from Anglican clerics threatened not only by Whitefield's popularity but also by his direct attacks on any fellow ministers he believed unregenerate. "O pity, pity the church of England," he would cry. "See how too, too many of her sons are fallen from her articles, and preach themselves, not Christ Jesus the Lord. . . . Arise, arise, and be not of the number of those who only fleece their flocks."[32] If they did not proclaim themselves "born again," Whitefield considered them far from God. The controversy heightened the press coverage, and his reputation preceded his arrival in America in May 1738.

The young preacher had an immediate impact on the colony. Stephens delightedly noticed "the most thronged Congregation I had ever seen here" for Whitefield's first service. Just five days later, less happily, he noted the beginnings of a more intense disrespect accorded the Georgia magistrates. "One Pat Grant . . . affronted the Magistrates, by peremptorily refusing to obey their Orders, and setting them in open Contempt for which they very deservedly committed him to Gaol." The following day, a "Great Stir made in Behalf of Pat Grant by his Countrymen" did not bring about his release, but over the next two weeks, Stephens's journal reveals in turn Whitefield's ever-increasing audiences and the local population's ever-increasing refusal to defer to their social betters. The timing of social change was striking. The congregation exceeded the capacity of the church by early June; by the end of the month, "a Paper was fixed to the most publick Places, abusing the Magistrates in the most gross terms." It should come as no surprise that Grant died two years later in a duel with a gentleman from South Carolina, to whose social superiority he showed insufficient acknowledgment. "The poor people have been treated with great barbarity by their Carolina officers (after the manner of using their Negroes)."[33]

The pattern continued through July. "Mr. Whitfield gained more and more on the Affections of the People. . . . The Church wanted not a full Congregation before noon or after. . . . The publick Service well frequented." But Stephens the same month complained about how difficult controlling his labor force had become. His "own disorderly Servants . . . began to give more Trouble than my Son and I could readily dispense with."[34] The pastor left Savannah, briefly at first for a trip to Frederica, and then at the end of August, he returned to England. The disruptions did not immediately dissipate, for in September, Stephens described his servants as "false and lazy through the poisonous Influence of other idle Rascals" and complained that the free "common laboring People . . . required such Wages as is hardly to be believed."[35]

Insubordination toward the governing class was nothing new. But the previous three decades had seen a lull in direct or collective action in England and that which had occurred, such as that of the Waltham Blacks, met with new and severe oppressions. We cannot know all that Whitefield said in the Georgia pulpits that summer that helped push the poorer residents into action against figures of power and empowered them to demand fair market wages. However, the biggest clue may be found in his one direct reference to a biblical text he used. It was the short "First of St. James," which includes the passage, "let the brother of low degree rejoice, in that he is exalted; But the rich, in that he is made low: because as the flower of the grass he shall pass away. For the sun is no sooner risen with a burning heat, but it withereth the grass, and the flower thereof falleth, and the grace of the fashion of it perisheth: so also shall the rich man fade away in his ways."[36]

Perhaps, too, it was his support of education, because he opened schools in Savannah and neighboring villages, never a priority for southern planters. And we know Whitefield saw a direct link between economics and religion. After many travels, he would reflect upon the "state of religion" through the colonies. In Pennsylvania above all others, he believed "they have the Lord for their God," citing as evidence his observation that "there is a greater equality between the poor and the rich than perhaps can be found in any other place of the known world."[37]

We can also tell from the reactions to his sermons elsewhere around the Atlantic World that Whitefield acutely upset the Anglican hierarchy. His attacks on the established clergy were frequent and without mercy, comparing them to the Bible's Pharisees. Their responses revealed the extent to which religious and class structures were tied in the eighteenth century. The English church did not celebrate his winning of souls for the Lord; rather, they feared his appeal to the "illiterate Vulgar" who might easily become a "mob."[38] So although Whitefield never took on political authorities directly, the threat his popularity posed to the norms of civil society frightened many, especially those who wanted a compliant labor force.

■ Stephens finally grasped the connection between the full congregations of the summer and the disrespect accorded bosses around the colony when a new preacher took over Savannah's ministry in October. The contrast between his sermons and those of Whitefield led to disgruntled parishioners. "They thought he set too great a Value on good Works" and wanted a return to Whitefield's emphasis on "a sound Faith." As Stephens mulled the debate, he realized that the evangelist's theology did not emphasize the level of discipline he would have liked. "Such sublime Points in Divinity, I apprehend, are ill-suited with the present Circumstances of this young Colony, where the Preacher's Labour would most certainly be best bestowed, in plainly setting forth the sad Consequences of a vicious Life . . . and inculcating those Duties to God and our Neighbours, which are so essential in our Religion."[39] Like Wesley, Whitefield had made no call to a work ethic.

Perhaps Whitefield's successful conversions in Georgia—like Moll praying with the minister in Newgate—were not focused exactly on eternity. As his parishioners interpreted it, this version of God seemed all about turning the world upside down in the present. All winter long, Stephens battled with his own defiant servants and those of the Trust, who frequently ran away or refused to work. German servants, "having combined together," even made formal protests, claiming the demands on them were unjust. The magistrates found otherwise, ordering them to work on Saturdays to make up for the time they had spent on strike. Before the spring, according to Stephens, "the Plague of idle and roguish Servants was grown universal."[40]

The servants were not rebelling solely on philosophical grounds. A drought ruined another harvest, and by the spring of 1739, food shortages began to bite. In addition, colonial officials frequently called men away from their farms to drill and to build fortifications because of the threat of Spanish attack, as tensions between the European powers intensified. That threat only raised international prices for commodities, as ship captains ran higher risks at sea. So Thomas Causton spent much more than the Trustees had approved on purchasing food for the Public Stores from South Carolina and ship captains, upon which settlers depended for much of their needs. However, Causton's account keeping, or more accurately, lack thereof, completely aggravated the Trustees back in London. Confronted with a stack of bills for provisions, "all which profusion of Expence made the Gentlemen stare," they decided to rein in the storekeeper, severely curtailing all civil costs to explicitly stated items and demanding Causton send full and accurate accounts. Only servants of the Trust would receive sustenance from the Public Stores. Oglethorpe fired Causton in October.[41]

The winter of 1738–39 tried the spirits of even the most hardy when poor harvests and the dwindling food supplies from the Trust stretched the colony's resources (and its people) to their thinnest. As Whitefield himself noted in November, "Infant Georgia is an excellent soil for Christianity; you cannot live there without taking up a daily cross." Oglethorpe, usually an optimist, acknowledged "the lamentable State the colony was in." By December, the Trust's stores neared depletion. Some of the runaway servants fed themselves by hunting, both deer and cattle.[42]

The Malcontents marshaled the hunger and discontent of the fall of 1738 into a "Representation" in December: a petition that combined the poorer settlers' requests for new land-tenure regulations with their own for permission of slavery. Upon learning of restlessness among the Scottish Highlanders settled at Darien about tail-male tenure, the plea to the Trustees put the tenure issue first, "A free title, or fee-simple, to our lands . . . would . . . encourage those who remain here, cheerfully to proceed in making further improvements . . . as to make provisions for their posterity." The second request was for "the use of Negroes, with proper limitations." Those with planter aspirations told the craftsmen that slaves would be limited to unskilled labor, such as felling trees and caring for the rice crop, and so posed no threat to their livelihood. No one who had travelled to Charles Town, as Tailfer and his friends had, could think this enforceable, but the inclusion explains why the Malcontents could persuade so many Savannah tradesmen to sign on to the petition. One tradesman later reported to Egmont that he feared slaves "would take the Work out of white Mens hands, and so impoverish them, as is the case in Charlestown, where the tradesmen are all beggars," but that the Malcontents had "prevailed on others to sign by assuring them there should not be above 2 or three Negroes to one white man." Even with this promise of limitations on slave numbers, the poorer sort were very underrepresented on the petition: only nine servants among the 177 signees. And the Salzburgers of Ebenezer and the Highlanders of Darien refused to sign the Representation altogether because slavery would not solve their problems.[43]

The interests of the Darien community holding the defense line on the Florida frontier plus their masculine clan culture led their leader Mackintosh Mohr to present a petition refuting the Representation as the voice of all Georgians. Perhaps it is unlikely that all of the Highlanders truly subscribed to the notion that "it is shocking to human Nature, that any race of mankind and their Posterity should be sentenc'd to perpetual Slavery" as their petition declared, and perhaps the script was written by Oglethorpe. Yet even if they used the situation to negotiate for better supplies from the Trust, the essential argument they made that slavery would be of little benefit to their community made sense. Mohr had no loyalty to the Lowlanders, no money to purchase slaves, and no use for a labor force that might turn on his people, already concerned with the Spanish. "How miserable would it be to us . . . to have one enemy without, and a more dangerous one in our Bosoms!"[44]

The Salzburgers also responded, condemning the Malcontent Representation. Unlike the Darien petition, there would be no philosophical opposition to slavery. Instead, they rejected slavery for very practical and sometimes racist reasons. They feared enslaved Africans and believed them to be liable to violence at any time, arguing that "White People are in Danger of Life because of them." It is not clear if the Salzburgers thought it was the enslavement, the Africanness, or the non-Protestant status that was the root of the violence. (Slaves were alternately assumed to be Moors and therefore Muslim or associated with the Catholic powers, equally sinister to eighteenth-century Pietists.) The petition also ridiculed the argument that Europeans were incapable of farming in the South. "We laugh at such a Talking," they wrote, claiming they had produced a surplus.[45]

Oglethorpe wrote personally to his fellow Trustees, dismissing the Representation as the work of Tailfer's brother-in-law Robert Williams in particular, who apparently told many he would extend credit for the opportunity to buy slaves to those who would put their land up as collateral. "This may turn to his advantage as a Negro merchant," noted Oglethorpe, "but all the labouring poor white men will be starved by it." In a second letter, the general included some measure of concern for the people who would stand to lose most. "We should occasion the misery of thousands in Africa, by setting men upon using arts to buy and bring into perpetual slavery the poor people who now live free there."[46]

While the Representation and counterpetitions crossed the Atlantic, Savannah residents continued to deal with the food shortage. Restrictions on tenure seemed moot as fall turned into winter and the situation deteriorated. On February 1, 1739, came the announcement that there was no meat left in the Public Stores and not much of anything else. The citizens confronted Stephens with a barrage of complaints wherever he went, arguing for the slaughter of Trust cattle, but Stephens wanted Oglethorpe to make that call. Soon, the cattleman took it upon himself to butcher "one of the largest steers of the Trustees." A few weeks later, a new storekeeper consented to killing another dozen cattle, but not enough to prevent a couple of servants, "young Rogues," according to Stephens, from stealing and butchering a bullock belonging to one of the magistrates. Their only defense was that they "were tempted to this from a Desire of fresh Meat." By the end of March, Stephens admitted that Savannah's population thinned as runaways took off into the woods or Charles Town.[47] "Disobedient" German Trust servants were "punished with . . . the withholding of their provisions . . . as a result they go out to hunt and fish."[48]

Although it appeared the colony was failing, the introduction of slavery offered no solace to the poor, who would never have the wherewithal to buy them, and so the Malcontents saw no further growth in their movement, despite the worsening conditions. The Trustees, having had Stephens inform them of the situation in Savannah, responded by dismantling what there was of a coalition. They told Stephens to announce a forthcoming change in the tenure regulations that would allow freeholders to give land by deed or will to their daughters. The official reply to the Representation reminded the workers and farmers of the consequences of the introduction of slavery. "The colony would soon be too like its neighbours, void of white inhabitants, filled with blacks, and reduced to be the precarious property of a few." In a prophetic phrase, the Trustees described South Carolina's slaves as "the terror of their unadvised masters," three months before the Stono Rebellion. Their argument appeared to gather some momentum; by the following summer, Stephens claimed "few now were for having Negroes."[49]

Gradually the congregation drifted away from church services over the course of the winter, until by February 1739, "the Ministry itself rather seemed to be set at naught by too many, partly such as being Protestants of a different Persuasion . . . and partly others, who made little Show of any Religion at all."[50] Yet when (premature) word of Whitefield's return delighted the townspeople in June, Stephens found it "a Matter of more Indifference." To Stephens, the pastor did not represent an ally in good government of the lower orders, in the normal manner of Anglican ministers.

And good government Georgia needed, apparently, for the upending of the social order was not limited to uppity male servants. Women increasingly refused to observe their place, to Stephens's distaste and dismay. Perhaps they were listening to Moll's plea for female autonomy, "Let the Ladies see that the Advantage is not so much on the other Side as the men think it is . . .'Tis nothing but . . . the fear of not being Marry'd at all, and of that frightful State of Life, call'd *an old Maid* . . . This I say, is the Woman's Snare; but would the Ladies once but get above that Fear and manage rightly."[51] The relative lack of marriageable-age women gave females negotiating power should they adopt Moll's attitude. The rapidity with which widows remarried—much faster than others around the colonies in the eighteenth century—indicates few had Moll's chutzpah. But those who carried themselves with self-confidence and understood how to maneuver in a liminal borderland aggravated Stephens.[52]

From the beginning, Mary Musgrove Matthews Bosomworth used her abilities to speak both English and Creek to make herself indispensable to Oglethorpe and the colony in general, but maintained a position independent of the Trustees. A succession of husbands came and went, but she thrived and continued to jealously guard her autonomy. She claimed that Tomochichi had granted her three of the coastal islands in 1737, and despite heavy opposition from Trustees and their officials, would not relent on her land claims for over twenty years. Eventually she would be recognized as owner of one of the most beautiful spots in North America, St. Catherines Island.[53]

Mrs. Jane Camuse became the chief silk producer for the colony after the death and departure of the Italian Amatis brothers. Much had been made of Georgia's supposed ability to compete with global producers of silk, and the Trustees harped on it for years, offering bounties and refusing to surrender this goal in the face of endless evidence that silk manufacture would never constitute a growing concern on the frontier. They had helped justify parliamentary financial support for the colony by promising a commodity the Empire did not produce elsewhere.[54] Growing the mulberry trees was not the problem. But the slow, gentle gathering of the leaves to feed the silkworms and the intricate and constant process of caring for the worms and their eggs required an expert. The value of silk came from this specialized knowledge, and observers noted that she had "an exceeding fine hand" at silk production. Like Mary Musgrove, Camuse quickly grasped her value and jealously protected her interests. When the Trustees repeatedly told Oglethorpe and Stephens to make sure Camuse had apprentices, she often defiantly negotiated for a higher salary. Somehow, none of her apprentices ever really learnt the skills she supposedly taught.[55]

Refusing to be bound by any social mores about female behavior, she proved willing to be perceived as obstreperous, arguing loudly and often with Stephens when demanding her pay. "We have been subject to the unlimited Demands of a Woman, who set too great a Value on herself, to admit of any Repulse." Like any good capitalist, Camuse actually set exactly the value on her expertise the market would bear, but with the current gender and class relations, elite men in the eighteenth century could not stomach this reality. The Trustees began advising Stephens look elsewhere for someone with her skills, "for there must be some Checque to Mrs. Camus's extraordinary Demand, to prevent her overvaluing her Self." The discussion continued for years in letters sailing back and forth across the Atlantic. "This unparalled behaviour of hers; who knowing too well the English of sine Qua non, finds it in her power to set what value on herself she pleases; & without Remorse, usurps the Quality of a Mistress, where a gratefull Obedience as a Servant . . . would better become her," William Stephens bitterly complained. Why would this woman not accept her place?[56]

Mrs. Avery, widow of the surveyor and mapmaker of the colony, wrote directly to Egmont and the Trustees to demand an adequate price for the map she had in her possession. Stephens found her to have an "inflexible Disposition," but she secured most of what she wanted. Other women testing the limits of the possible included Ellen Dean, "fyn'd for defamation"; Elizabeth Cundall, who ran a "bawdy house"; and Mary Hodges-Townsend, who operated one of the Malcontents' favorite taverns; whereas Elizabeth Penrose (along with a husband ten years her junior), did both, thereby earning the title "Conqueror Over the whole place" from one frustrated man. The most interesting women were those who defied conventions about being submissive to their husbands. No fear of the "Old Maid" label bothered Margaret Bright who left her husband or Elizabeth Hughes, who, having survived two husbands, decided she would prefer to just live with her next lover rather than commit to marriage. Hannah Willoughby attracted the attentions of four different men in the 1730s, three of whom married her, the other "bought her for a shillin."[57]

But one unnamed woman above all represented the possibilities of a frontier colony. A certain Captain Davis from South Carolina operated several vessels and traded with the Caribbean islands and Florida. By May 1739, he had decided to make Savannah his home base and seemed destined to be the leading merchant of the port. Embracing the autocratic mentalité of his planter brethren, Davis refused to acknowledge any authority but his own. He would trade with St. Augustine even when Britain and Spain were at war. But, according to Stephens, "his most visible Foible, was keeping a Mulatto Servant (or Slave) who in Reality was his Mistress." This very public relationship did not merely counter racial sexual boundaries. Stephens acknowledged not only her "exceeding fine Shape," but her expertise in running Davis's business. Davis's career had left him physically disabled, and his partner not only took care of his personal needs but had gradually learned to keep his accounts, until Davis "suffered almost every Thing to pass through her Hands . . . She had the Custody of all his Cash."[58]

Mrs. Davis, as she was in all but name, made it perfectly clear to all who came in contact with her that they "were expected not to treat her with Contempt." When one of Davis's shipmasters failed to show appropriate respect, she responded with disdain for him and in anger he slapped her face. Davis would brook no "Abuse of Madam," and despite his value as an experienced sailor, the disrespectful shipmaster lost his command of the snow.[59]

■ Captain Davis had recently faced disrespect from a different source. The Spanish Crown's 1693 offer of freedom to any slave who might escape from an English colony had tempted unfree Carolinians for decades. Joining Spanish and Yamasee warriors on raids on outlying South Carolina plantations, they were the scourge of the planter class. The Crown's offer was renewed and well publicized in 1733, and the numbers of freedmen grew so quickly that the governor of Florida established Fort Mosa (often called Moosa by Georgians; now known as Mose) as a free black settlement charged with holding New Spain's first line of defense in the event of an attack by the British mainland colonials. As that attack seemed likely to come in the form of their old plantation masters, the ex-slaves were only too delighted to volunteer to guard the border.[60] No planter endured bigger losses than Davis. A group including nineteen of his slaves had requisitioned his boat and "run away from him . . . all at once" in 1738. Davis traveled down to Florida to claim them from his Spanish trading partners, but faced only indignity in St. Augustine, where "all his said Negroes . . . laughed at him."[61]

In February 1739, the escape of more slaves southwards led to rumors of a vast conspiracy. As Stephens fearfully described, the plan was "to rise and forcibly make their way out of the Province . . . the Rising was to be universal." Four South Carolina planters rode through Savannah that month on their way to St. Augustine, hoping vainly for more luck than Davis. Another story of slave revolt circulated just over the Georgia line in the new community of Purrysburg. Savannah's residents found a Spanish spy "skulking in Town" in July, on his way back from Charles Town.[62] The white South nervously watched.

4

WHITEFIELD AND WAR, 1739–1742

The Wars and the Sea, and Trade, and other Incidents have
carried the Men so much away.
—Defoe, *Moll Flanders*

For the next few years, the internal fight for the political economy of the
colony took a backseat as events external to Savannah commanded the
attention and energies of the settlers. Kongolese warriors and Spanish soldiers in turn attacked the southern colonies, terrifying the British in
South Carolina and Georgia. The latter settlement went on a war footing
and eventually held the line, but the tragic cost extended beyond the lives
of the Highlanders who died protecting British claims in America. The
central purpose of the colony became murky for the Trustees. Caught up
in political wrangling and the intricacies of military budgets, many drifted
away from the Trust, while others took affront at the lack of deference
shown them by those on the ground in Georgia. Philanthropic gestures
gradually gave way to complaints about the uselessness of poor people. The
reality that those poor people worked very hard, proving essential to the
war effort in Frederica, went unnoticed by policy makers, who heard only
from planters and their lobbyist. Poor whites had no representative in
London.[1]

The Spanish had not welcomed Oglethorpe's settlement in Georgia,
arguing correctly that their claim to the region was recognized by previous treaties. But the boundary line was a relatively minor irritant in a
litany of issues between Spain and Britain in the 1730s, mostly concerning international trade practices. Prime Minister Robert Walpole neither
desired war nor harbored any loyalty to Georgia, considering the new
colony merely a pawn in the grand scheme of global commerce. The
Trustees, however, found support from leading and fiercely nationalistic
politicians, who seized on this foreign policy opportunity to weaken the
once-almighty Walpole. As tensions mounted, the king appointed Oglethorpe commander-in-chief of not only Georgia, but also the Carolinas
in June 1737. Then members of the House of Commons witnessed the jar
containing the pickled ear of British mariner Robert Jenkins, cut off

(seven years earlier) by a Spanish captain, an incident they could turn to great use in amassing popular support for war. In January 1739, Anglo-Spanish negotiations produced an agreement that did not eliminate Spanish right of search and seizure and did not firmly guarantee Georgia for the British. An outcry in Parliament followed, with William Pitt calling the settlement a "national ignominy." Under severe pressure that summer, Walpole decided to renew armed hostilities with Spain and dispatched a fleet toward the West Indies.[2]

The Spaniards brashly sent an emissary to South Carolina's slaves, "a Negro that spoke English very well," in a boat captained by Don Pedro, an officer from St. Augustine, who pretended he was lost and looking for Oglethorpe when approached by whites. Spreading the word about freedom in Florida, the boat stopped at many spots. The Spaniard caught in Savannah in July no doubt served the same mission: to raise recruits for the Spanish cause among the enslaved in the British colonies.[3]

On September 9, in Stono, near Charles Town, a group led by Catholic Kongolese and other warriors struck out for freedom. Determined to rescue others from the degradations of slavery, they risked everything by stopping at several plantations en route, killing the whites and offering to liberate the enslaved, rather than moving more quickly and silently to free only themselves. Marching through South Carolina on their way to Fort Mosa, banging a drum in America's first liberty parade, they rescued somewhere between eighty and one hundred souls.[4] But they never made it to Florida.

Their daring bid for liberty was foiled by a group of planters on horseback who raised the alarm, and many of the escapees were hunted down over the next few days and weeks, "some hang'd and some Gibbet'd alive." As a deterrent to others hoping to flee south, "the Planters . . . Cutt off their heads and set them up at every Mile Post they came to." A messenger to Savannah delivered the news on September 13, offering a reward of fifty pounds for any slave caught and returned alive to Charles Town and twenty-five for dead bodies.[5]

Georgia official William Stephens wanted to help, but had to admit that the colony "could ill spare any of the few men we had, that were fit to bear Arms, and by so doing leave ourselves more and more defenseless."[6] Able-bodied young men had found employment in the war effort. Neither Oglethorpe nor the Salzburgers, scared as they were of "gangs" of desperate refugees, sympathized with the planters of Charles Town. "Mr. Oglethorpe told us here that the misfortune with the Negro rebellion had begun on the day of the Lord, which these slaves must desecrate with work and in other ways at the desire, command and compulsion of their masters and that we could recognize a *jus talionis* [eye for an eye justice] in it."[7] The Stono Rebellion admonished the Carolina planter class only enough that their new Negro Act of 1740 tightened the screws on slave mobility. They also felt it necessary to correct the demographic imbalance by limiting slave imports during the 1740s. But the enormous profit margins available to those who will not pay their workers remained too tempting to substantially alter the mindset of the Masters of the Universe. Some of those masters soon found themselves under the military command of Oglethorpe in the siege of St. Augustine.

War with the Spanish was officially declared in October. Oglethorpe's focus turned entirely away from the philanthropic vision with which he had founded Georgia and onto his other passion: the quest for military glory. He had served against the Turks as a young man, and like a typical eighteenth-century gentleman, Oglethorpe loved the uniforms and medals, the gallantry, and the adventure offered by escapades abroad. The rest of his life was given over to these pursuits. But his attitude to the South Carolina planters would interfere with his capacity to conduct his military missions. His appointment as commander included £1,000 of salary that would otherwise have lined the pockets of the new South Carolina governor, James Glen. The planters of that colony were "stark mad" that they might be expected to make up the difference in their governor's salary. Resentful, too, that he prevented the expansion of slavery and that he treated them as provincials rather than acknowledge their aristocratic pretensions, South Carolina's officers nursed their grievances throughout the Florida campaign. They abused the poor white men of Georgia placed under their command, "after the manner of using their Negroes."[8] When British forces failed to capture St. Augustine's fortress, the planters would put the blame fully on Oglethorpe's shoulders.

Oglethorpe arrived at Frederica in September 1738 with a regiment of 700 men. "We want beer here extremely," he immediately reported to the Trustees. As tensions continued to ratchet up, serious preparations began in the summer of 1739 with a trip west of Augusta to negotiate support from southeastern Indians. Oglethorpe needed assurance that the Cherokees and Chickasaws would not ally with the Spaniards and that promise did not come cheaply. The Creeks also secured lucrative military contracts for providing horses as well as warriors for the forthcoming hostilities. Savannah's residents were warned they went unarmed into the woods "at their own Peril," but many were less frightened than delighted at the opportunities to profit from the British army's need for local knowledge. Preparations in the southernmost towns continued into the new year. Darien's streets emptied as the Highlanders headed to Frederica, where Oglethorpe could offer a secure supply of food and the chance of combat. Unsanitary conditions were the norm on the era's military bases, so to combat dysentery, the Trustees dispatched "a Bottle of Salitrum Seeds for the Bloody Flux," believed to be "a sure remedy." Unfortunately, soldiers did not get the instructions that "it is best for the Patient to take a Vomit first," before using the seeds until three years later.[9]

Oglethorpe amassed a force of at least 1,500 British regulars, Highlanders, South Carolina militia, and Creek Indians. The navy committed seven warships. Some served more patriotically than others. The South Carolina Assembly believed correctly that the Spanish had no inclination to attack Charles Town "but as that Garrison [St. Augustine], even in Times of Peace, was a continual Receptacle of criminal and fugitive Slaves," they did have a dog in the fight. And in the event of war, perhaps the Stono experience might be magnified, and "what Resistance could a thin . . . Colony make to a Foe without, when they had such numerous and cruel ones within, at whose Mercies the Lives of their Families must lie." (With a self-deluding twist, masters would ease their conscience by referring to their slaves as cruel and as people upon whose mercy they depended!) Still, they only agreed to send men and materiel if Oglethorpe could assure them of a high probability of success.[10]

In January, a large raiding party of Creeks, Chickasaws, and Uchizes accompanied by some of the Georgia Rangers won the small Spanish outposts of Pupo and Picolata, west of St. Augustine. Perhaps the relatively easy fall of these forts made Oglethorpe overly confident about his mission to take St. Augustine. His expedition set off in May 1740, seizing Fort Diego on the St. John's River and establishing base there. Oglethorpe led a reconnaissance mission several days later, right up to the thick walls of the St. Augustine Castillo, taking and damaging Fort Mosa on the way. His troop retreated to St. John's to plan the siege. (See Map 2.)[11]

While the main body of Oglethorpe's troops would lay siege to St. Augustine, and the warships under the command of Commodore Pearse should prevent relief by sea, a lightly armed, mobile force of approximately 150 men were to hold the countryside, patrolling for any Spaniards who might surreptitiously attempt to secure food. Jealousies between officers Palmer and Mackay, whose commands overlapped, immediately came to the fore. Centuries-old ethnic loyalties plagued the expedition; a year even before any action, English officers complained bitterly about the Scottish.[12] With the Scottish Highlanders, who composed the largest component,

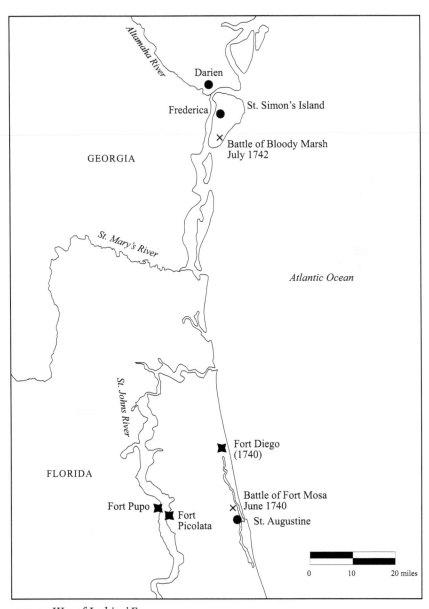

MAP 2. *War of Jenkins' Ear*

following Mackay's orders and the English Carolinians behind Palmer, the unit failed to gel. Although Oglethorpe warned them to elude counter-raids by the Spanish, specifying they should not camp twice in the same spot, the troop quickly set up camp at Fort Mosa on June 10. Firing and burning houses in the town of Augustine, they supported the bombardment by the main force for the next few days.[13]

The commander of St. Augustine felt the pressure. At dawn on June 15, about 300 Spanish forces attacked Mosa, including ex-slaves who had escaped Carolinian plantations. Caught off guard, soldiers scurrying for clothing and weapons, the British were soundly defeated, with three-quarters of the Highlanders dead or captured, leaving Darien a town of widows.[14]

Despite this huge blow to the morale of Oglethorpe's party, the siege of Augustine continued for three more weeks and came close to starving out the people sheltered in the Castillo. But the British could not entirely secure the region, and in early July, a flotilla of vessels from Cuba smuggled provisions into the fort. Oglethorpe and his naval officers conferred about the logistics of maintaining the siege, with Commodore Pearse arguing that the onset of hurricane season in the region made the situation too dangerous to sustain. The British retreated to Frederica.[15]

The military adventure only exacerbated Savannah's struggles. The poor may have enjoyed the liberty of controlling their own destiny, but in this time of war, they worried about their next meal. Oglethorpe's report of October 1738 warned the Trustees of "nothing but destruction to the Colony, unless some assistance be immediately sent," but communication took months to reach London. By March 1739, the Trustees had heard so many dire stories that, having battled for £20,000 from Parliament, they decided to relent on the supply of provisions and sent flour, cheese, butter, and beef as quickly as possible.[16] But most members of Parliament supported Georgia now solely for imperial defense. The philanthropic gaze seemed to evaporate for all but Egmont and a very few Trustees. Over the course of 1739, attendance at Trustee meetings dropped off, and discussions centered around either the machinations for and against Walpole's ministry or how to curtail Oglethorpe's lavish expenditures. In their opinion, the general did not appropriately mark the distinction between military and civil budgets. By January 1740, they had cut Oglethorpe off from any access to the Trust's finances.

Some of the loss of faith in Georgia's mission to relieve the lot of England's poor stemmed from the arrival of Thomas Stephens in London in October 1739. The son of Trustee official William Stephens, Thomas had been wooed by the Malcontents and would spend the next few years serving as their chief lobbyist in London. At first, he approached Egmont in hopes of persuading the Trustee leader that the idea of prohibiting slavery had been flawed. Making no headway there, Stephens began a whispering campaign all over London, circulating the 1738 Representation and maintaining a flow of pamphlets and memorials designed to discredit the Trustees and Oglethorpe in particular. Settlers had abandoned Georgia, he claimed; only the regiment remained. Egmont despaired at his inability to counter the misinformation. "We were now almost entirely sunk in our credit with the King, the Ministry, the Parliament, the City, & the Kingdom."[17]

Although Savannah certainly had not been deserted, none of its residents prospered and morale plummeted. The Malcontents prepared to abandon their lands. The only bright spot on the horizon was the rumor of Whitefield's return. In fact, Whitefield did not reach American shores until the late fall of 1739, and he toured the northern colonies before returning to Savannah. His fame in the interval had grown enormously. When Church of England ministers prevented him from using their pulpits, he responded by preaching in the fields, attracting huge crowds and more publicity. The bishop of London issued a pastoral letter condemning his practice, but the crowds did not diminish. Now the colonies' first celebrity, he continued the practice throughout Pennsylvania and New York in November and December, building a revival on a scale that astonished all who observed or participated. Benjamin Franklin, skeptical at first, quickly understood that Whitefield was a phenomenon and offered to publish his sermons and journals, helping to further the celebrity status of the young cleric. In the colonies, as in Britain, established clergy reacted with animosity to the threat he posed to their authority.[18]

Any Children, as such are generally unprovided for, by the
Poverty or Forfeiture of their Parents, so they are immediately
taken into the Care of the Government, and put into a
Hospital call'd the House of Orphans.
—Defoe, *Moll Flanders*

Throughout England and the mid-Atlantic colonies, Whitefield's barnstorming generated collections for Georgia's orphans.[19] The Trustees had officially appointed him Savannah's minister in December 1738 and granted 500 acres for the orphanage, while donors of every class opened their pockets, even the poor. "They give their mites for the orphan house with a cheerful and ready heart," wrote Whitefield. Although he remained devoted to that cause, gradually he saw his American mission as something larger than the parish church in Savannah. As he received the adulation of large numbers in Philadelphia, the idea of serving by leading a transatlantic revival took hold, and before he had ever returned to the new colony, he sought a substitute for his weekly duties. "I should rejoice, if you would come and supply my place at Savannah," he asked a friend back in Oxford. To another he explained his intentions: "If I resigned the parish, I shall be more at liberty to take a tour around America."[20] This decision to cast off the appointment would not earn him any fans among the Trustees in future years. Whitefield cared little, however, and struck out as an independent, preaching wherever and whenever he desired; "the whole world is now my parish," he declared. Everywhere he went, however, he collected funds for the Georgia orphans.[21]

Upon his heralded return to Savannah in January 1740, while Oglethorpe was building his force at Frederica, George Whitefield rescued the adult settlers left in Savannah as well as the orphans. He immediately set about hiring labor and harboring those in distress, quickly becoming the patron of almost the entire town, although his young assistant James Habersham took care of many of the logistics and practicalities of the project. Whitefield observed that the previous year or two had seen a decline in Savannah's population, as military service and tough times had driven people away from the city. Paying generous wages, he employed over forty people to build the main house named Bethesda, so that, as Stephens recorded, "there was hardly one Sawyer of any Value in Town, but all hired, and engaged by him . . . Most of our Carpenters, Bricklayers, etc were likewise engaged by him."[22] He also hired agricultural laborers to cut wood and plant crops, while women were set to spinning and weaving the necessary textiles. With close to forty orphans living in the house by the end of February added to the upkeep of his adult workforce, Whitefield claimed to be feeding one hundred people per day.[23] By July, Stephens reported "a grand edifice," surrounded by six "good, handsome" outbuildings. The expense of such maintenance would keep much of Whitefield's time focused on fund-raising for years to come, while Habersham stayed in Bethesda trying to sustain the institution through farming and silk production.[24]

The high wages he proved willing to pay did not endear Whitefield to the Malcontents, for again the meddling preacher disrupted their desire for a cheap labor force. Nor did his critiques of the lifestyles and culture of wealthy planters all over the South. Traveling through Maryland and Virginia, he had visited several plantations and did not refrain from calling out plantation mistresses on the "vanity of their false politeness." Masters who prevented their slaves from spending time in religious worship were compared to Old Testament villains. "Their masters, Pharaoh like, cry out 'Ye are idle, ye are idle,'" Whitefield wrote his fellow awakener, Gilbert Tennent, wondering if they could ever make a difference in the slave societies. "In these parts Satan seems to lead people captive at his will."[25] Long a critic of horse racing, card playing, and other planter amusements, the gracious living and charm of southern plantations would not beguile the preacher.

Certainly the religious tradition of the Tidewater South bore little resemblance to the New England colonies or Quaker Pennsylvania. While small pockets of Calvinists and Quakers tried to build a following, religious mission did not push the original settlement of the great slave societies of Virginia and South Carolina. Virginia's seventeenth-century governor, William Berkeley, vehemently opposed teaching people to read their Bibles. Schools bring disobedience, he said, for a plantation order with an oligarchy commanding a huge unfree labor force, whether slave or indentured servant, did not want literate workers questioning authority. As the southern colonies grew and the elite prospered, the Anglican church bolstered planter control. The great planters chose the ministers, who emphasized God's love for order and the predestination not only of the afterlife but of the present social structure. Pew placement reflected social rank. According to Whitefield, the Maryland government overpaid the clerics, "by giving them too much tobacco," collected as a tithe from "every person taxable . . . though great numbers never hear or see them." Church services by the eighteenth century were a social event in Charles Town, as carriages, thoroughbreds, and silk gowns and elaborate bonnets paraded their owners' wealth. "I question whether the court-end of London could exceed them in affected finery, gaiety of dress and a deportment ill-becoming persons who have had such Divine judgments lately sent among them," commented Whitefield, referring to the Stono Rebellion. But he felt his interpretation of that event as a message from God failed to make an impact on the planters of Charles Town. "Thus it was with Pharoah [sic] and the Egyptians," he reflected later.[26] Men frequently chatted casually throughout the services about gambling on the horse races planned for the afternoon, or bragged on their sexual escapades with their slave concubines.[27]

Methodist and Pietist conceptions of the lowly Christ aiding the poor, throwing the moneylenders from the Temple, and blasting the Pharisees' arrogance glaringly contrasted with Anglican cosmology and planters' conspicuous consumption.[28] And for that reason, most of the Awakening's itinerant preachers would be forcibly kept out of the Tidewater South until the 1760s. So it is fascinating to observe George Whitefield himself in the very midst of that world and to grasp how this man who *never* directly challenged the political authorities' right to govern or their right to own slaves constituted such a serious menace to their way of life.

Whitefield set off for Charleston for a few days in March 1740 and was warmly received at dissenting churches, but not in the Anglican pulpits. Already, Alexander Garden, the Anglican commissary for South Carolina, was aware of the reputation of the evangelist and his penchant for holding ministers accountable to the Gospel. Garden had welcomed Whitefield on his original trip two years before, but now went on the offensive, condemning Whitefield's disrespect for other clergymen and depicting him as the Pharisee. Anglican clergymen also objected to the sense of spiritual superiority these "born-again" Methodists emanated, so sure of their own place in heaven, while calling out other ministers. Nonetheless, Whitefield managed to raise £70 for the orphanage that weekend; apparently plenty of people ignored Garden's warning.[29]

Among those undaunted by Garden were Hugh and Catherine Bryan, a wealthy planter couple. Unable to attend any of the services, they made a special trip to meet Whitefield at the orphanage in June. Catherine did not live much longer, but her widower would become a devoted believer in the New Birth philosophy. That Whitefield had recently launched a fierce attack upon planters in general did not deter Hugh Bryan; rather, he accepted his teacher's admonitions and changed his habits to a degree that shook South Carolina planter society.[30]

Whitefield's attack, fired up by the established church's opposition, came in the form of an open letter to *The Inhabitants of Maryland, Virginia, and North and South Carolina concerning Their Negroes,* presented to Benjamin Franklin in the spring of 1740 for publication and widespread distribution around the American colonies. The letter did not call for emancipation; rather, Whitefield complained of the brutal treatment of slaves and asserted that the planters should allow them to practice their faith. "God has a quarrel with you for your cruelty to the poor negroes," he chastised the southerners, pointing out that they treated their horses and dogs better than their workers. He compared the mealtimes of masters "faring sumptuously" with the insufficient nutrition accorded slaves, "notwithstanding most of the comforts you enjoy were solely owing to their indefatigable labours." Citing the book of James, he predicted divine punishment.[31]

The entire biblical passage, from James 5, bears quoting to explain Whitefield's judgment of planter values and the unbridled opposition he kindled in the southern elite: "Go to now, ye rich men, weep and howl for your miseries that shall come upon you. Your riches are corrupted, and your garments are motheaten. Your gold and silver is cankered; and the rust of them shall be a witness against you, and shall eat your flesh as if it were fire. Ye have heaped treasure together for the last days. Behold, the hire of the labourers who have reaped down your fields, which is of you kept back by fraud, crieth: and the cries of them which have reaped are entered into the ears of the Lord of Sabaoth. Ye have lived in pleasure on the earth, and been wanton."[32] This epistle by James is believed to be the first of the New Testament and reflects the philosophy of the early church so revered by Wesley and Whitefield. The potential political consequences of a minister reading such passages from the pulpit horrified the gentry.

But Whitefield did not stop there. "Think you, your children are in any way better by nature than the poor negroes? No! In no wise!" That he meant only the equality of their souls mattered little because such a challenge to white supremacy had rarely been publicly voiced in the eighteenth-century American colonies. Coming less than a year after Stono's rebellious slaves had marched from plantation to plantation proclaiming "Liberty!," Whitefield threatened the whole lucrative business of slavery by denying God's endorsement of racial and class hierarchies. He had no conscious intention of doing any such thing; Whitefield later supported the introduction of slavery into Georgia and would purchase several people to labor at the orphanage in the 1750s.[33] His pronouncements consistently alluded to spiritual rather than material affairs. But his audiences of every rank translated his biblical references into matters political, and to colonial elites, especially those of the South, he represented a dangerous ideology of equality. Class equality threatened their privilege no less than racial equality and perhaps more because a servant who might quote holy scripture would be less compliant than an African to whom such defenses were out of reach.

That Savannah's population decreased during the war years is without dispute. Best estimates see the town's population down to two hundred at its lowest point. The disruption in food supply caused by the closure of the stores and the decline in agricultural production resulting from military service made these the leanest years in the city's history. Out-migration to other colonies was not uncommon. But by the spring of 1740, while Whitefield revitalized the Savannah community spiritually and materially, the other settlements around the colony were thriving. Oglethorpe's military budget guaranteed plentiful supplies in the southern parts, supplemented by Darien's cattle and the bountiful fish. Whitefield described walking in Ebenezer "near 4 miles in one continued field, with a most plentiful crop of corn, pease & potatoes."[34]

The town growing around the Indian trading post at Augusta was also "flourishing," a frontier multicultural community quite distinct in atmosphere from Savannah. The residents spread their homes out along the river, rather than in a grid system, and had crops enough in 1740 to aid Savannah's hungry. Richard Kent, captain in the Georgia Rangers, stayed on in his dual role as military and civilian commander of the town through the war years, with the chief task of maintaining positive relations with neighboring Creeks, Cherokees, and especially Squirrel King's band of Chickasaws. Using Chickasaw intelligence, he countered French propaganda attempting to lure the loyalty of the Creek warriors and hunters. As Kent adopted a laissez-faire attitude to the business community, the traders watched the Indians and learned how their interests were best served by playing off one powerful European state against another. While the Creeks would use the competition between the English and French to extract the best prices, the traders secured licenses from both South Carolina and Georgia and cited whichever authority suited them at any given moment. Gradually over the 1740s, they would realize that cooperation benefited them (if not their suppliers or customers) more than competition, and leading traders organized a monopoly company, Brown, Rae and Company. Certainly many in Augusta appeared to be weathering the worst of Georgia's starving days.[35]

Should word of this commercial success reach England, perhaps the Trustees' plan would merit praise and support, thwarting the Carolina planters' expansionist schemes. The alternative society taking shape in Georgia converted the planters' fury into action. They needed a public relations strategy, one that would discredit the Trustees, particularly Oglethorpe, and depict a colony on the brink of collapse. In July 1740, the South Carolina Assembly appointed a committee of enquiry into the failure to take Augustine, and their report a year later hammered Oglethorpe hard in an autopsy of the campaign. Finally released in a public pamphlet in 1742, the report slammed Oglethorpe's ego as the main culprit in the fiasco. "His Name, in his own Opinion, was to produce a Surrender, the landing on Anastasia, which no Body disputed, was the *Conquest of Anastasia*, the coming to Moosa after Palmer's defeat was the *Retaking of Moosa*—from no Body too."[36]

In Savannah, the Malcontents desperately tried to recruit followers, sponsoring horse races as a community gathering where they appealed to locals on the tenure issue. Whitefield's blend of employment and philosophy curtailed their appeal, however, and by the end of the summer, Tailfer and many of the other leaders packed their belongings for a new start in Charles Town. Their incessant claim that profit was impossible in Georgia proved groundless when Robert Williams, an Atlantic merchant, who sought a market for the slaves he could ship to Savannah, admitted that his lumber shipments from Georgia "had a gain . . . although he paid 3 shillings a day to hired labourers to cut it." The reality was that, as in the northern colonies, opportunities abounded in the colony for commercial profits. Those profits might not rival the riches garnered from workers held captive or the sale of children to the highest bidder. They would suffice to create a free society, however, where people of all ranks could achieve a competency, supporting a family with a degree of financial security unavailable in England and the potential for greater rewards for those prepared to take risks. But no one called the concept of equality of opportunity a self-evident truth; that idea belonged to a revolution that had not yet occurred. Eighteenth-century aristocrats held no moral qualms about social hierarchies with themselves at the top of the pyramid. Anything else constituted anarchic democracy. With such beliefs, they salved their consciences.[37]

South Carolina's Stono Rebellion had set the Malcontents' cause backward; now Whitefield's renewal of the settlers threatened their plans. With Methodist theology magnifying class identity rather than racial identity, the time had come to abandon the quest to create a unified white appeal for slavery in Georgia. From the comfort of Charles Town, a "Land of Liberty" as they described it, they would manage the campaign against the Trustees. Warning travelers passing through Charles Town in the fall of 1740 that only lunatics went to Savannah, they sent Bolzius and others letters filled with bogus assertions about Georgia reverting to the Spanish if slavery remained illegal.[38]

Their campaign mainly focused on convincing members of Parliament that the colony was poorly managed by the Trustees. Thomas Stephens had failed to persuade Egmont of the need for a change in labor restrictions. He and Robert Williams now lobbied for an inquiry into management of the colony, mentioning that "a Sect call'd Methodists contribute some what to the present distractions there."[39] The Trustees countered, explaining to friends in high places that the Malcontents composed only a small cabal. Undeterred, the Lowland Scots in Charles Town continued to pursue the introduction of slavery, with the publication of a pamphlet they hoped would circulate widely among the influential in London.[40]

In "A True and Historical Narrative of the Colony of Georgia," Tailfer and his friends opened with a heavily sarcastic ode to Oglethorpe as the "Author" of the colony's "Strength and Affluence, Freedom and Prosperity," thanking him for the gift of humility assured "by your Care to prevent our procuring, or so much as seeing, any *Negroes*." Money had been pointlessly spent on building Indian alliances, "those useless Vagrants," while half-starved English settlers suffered through "wasting and tormenting Fluxes" with only water to drink. They painted a picture of a dying colony, abandoned by all but corrupt officeholders of the Trust. Claiming the Trustees mismanaged the colony from the beginning, most of the narrative laid out accusations against the absolute authority of Causton and Oglethorpe. Piling on, they added that the dangerous Wesley apparently had used "*Jesuitical* Arts" to bring "a new kind of Tyranny." His spiritual efforts were "calculated to debase and depress the Minds of the People . . . and humble them with Fastings [and] Penances." They finished, however, by attributing the problems facing Georgia to one matter: "chiefly the denying the Use of Negroes." Conflating their own prosperity with that of the colony as a whole, the authors saw their inability to make Charles Town–sized profits without slavery as an indictment of the whole project.[41]

While Tailfer and his companions drew up their manuscript, Thomas Stephens relentlessly pushed the agenda in London. Rebuffed by Egmont again, he presented a memorial at the House of Commons. Although Egmont declared this pamphlet to be libelous, within weeks Parliament's debate over the annual allocation of funds to Georgia reflected Stephens's work. "The Trustees had been under a mistake in sending so many idle fellows from England to settle there, who would not labour here, and the Trustees might be assured would neither labour in Georgia," declared MP Sandys, his words to become fodder for historians ever since. The essential laziness of Savannah's residents became unquestioned, and the reality—that they worked efficiently and diligently for Whitefield and Williams when paid fair market wages—never gained any traction. No one represented the workers in Parliament. Even Oglethorpe, who so badly wanted the colony to succeed, was trapped by his class attitude into ranting that the "vile, disorderly, idle and shockingly rude" men of Savannah would not work for the wages he offered because "a diabolical spirit reign'd among them." The absence of deference infuriated him.[42]

In reality, fear of Spanish attack had led to population loss, as many households temporarily took shelter in South Carolina. The small community of Jews in Savannah, for example, fled at the very chance the Spanish might bring an Inquisition with them. But some returned and new emigrants arrived, so that by the time of the publication of the *Narrative*, the colony was growing again, without slavery. The Trustees' decision to amend tenures had "quelled the troublesome spirit," according to other informers. Recruiters in Germany and Scotland gathered hundreds of emigrants prepared to try their hand in Georgia.[43]

These numbers were not available in England, however. The propaganda war played out in coffee bars and on the floor of the House of Commons free from the stifling constraints of facts. The Trustees published and distributed their version of Georgia's development, explaining that those "Fluxes" had only been a problem at first, when the people had not realized that rum gives one a fever "and consequently a Flux" in southern latitudes. A lot had been learned since, apparently. They cited the Salzburgers' success and their appeals to the Trustees for further help for more of their countrymen. They included depositions from soldiers who had traveled both to southern Europe and Georgia, testifying "that the Peasants in Spain perform all the Works of Husbandry without the Assistance of Negroes." They outlined the recently authorized changes to tenure that now allowed female relatives to inherit. And they used considerable amounts of ink addressing the Malcontents' claim that only slavery would salvage the colony. The dreaded Spanish, who had in peacetime broadcast "Promises of Liberty," were now in open war along Georgia's border. How much more dangerous for every white person in Georgia could slaves be?[44]

But the Trustees' "Impartial Enquiry," as they entitled their report, so contrasted with that of Stephens that readers chose to believe whichever suited their philosophy. Finally, the House of Commons agreed to schedule an official hearing, and Thomas Stephens and Egmont each began to round up friendly witnesses, only to be frustrated by Walpole, who arranged for postponement after postponement. The prime minister's best interests were served by Georgia's murky status, as he wanted to keep the region a negotiable pawn in future diplomatic wrangles with Spain. One point brought full agreement from the MPs: George Whitefield should not be allowed to testify on anyone's behalf, as the "Enthusiastical Mad Man . . . would demean the dignity of the house." Stephens, after spreading rumors that Walpole prevented the hearings to protect his friends the Trustees, decided to update his employers in Charles Town. Egmont seethed.[45]

Many of the original Trustees had deserted the project by now. The second half of 1741 saw the last few dedicated philanthropists fight for the preservation of the colony as they had imagined it. In August and September, hundreds of new settlers congregated to set sail for Savannah. Upon the recommendations of ship captains, the Trustees decided to approve the lifting of the prohibition of rum, as they came to understand that it often served as currency in trade between the mainland and Caribbean colonies. Besides, "'tis the universal opinion in Georgia," reported a military officer back from the war, "that Rum punch is very wholsom, and would contribute to the health of the people." Even better than rum, the Trustees agreed to sponsor the passage of extra women with the hope that they would marry some of the soldiers serving with Oglethorpe and settle permanently. These measures might positively affect life in the colony, but the real fight about slavery would play out in London, where the voices of the English and German settlers were never heard.[46]

And the one who might have spoken for them, George Whitefield, only alienated the powerful. For the next few years, Whitefield made Bethesda his home base, but spent most of his time touring the northern colonies and Britain. Preaching to thousands, and with his sermons published by Franklin's presses, his fame kept growing, but so too did the controversy surrounding him, as Anglican authorities ramped up their campaign to discredit him and the other itinerants. In Charleston, Garden even charged Whitefield in ecclesiastical court with liturgical misbehavior, but this action only brought more press attention and more curious people to Whitefield's open air gatherings.[47]

However, while Whitefield's popularity with the general public exploded, he lost the confidence of the colony's officials. The Trustees had prohibited slavery not because of any belief in racial equality, but to force poor white people to work hard. William Stephens reported to them that Whitefield had declared in the Savannah church that "very few great and rich Men . . . could ever see Heaven." Although Stephens opposed the introduction of slavery, he, the Trustees, and the Malcontents shared class values. They all worried that Whitefield's message threatened the Georgian social order and took very seriously his disruption of both the normal work patterns and the subsequent upheaval in social relations in the colony. Something had to be done to curtail his influence over the colony's workers.[48]

Whitefield warned his followers to expect persecution from the powerful, "for Men in high Places would be offended at all Opposition made to their Delusions."[49] Proving him right, the rich men in high places in

London set about reducing the preacher's power. Concerned for the children in his care, some who were not even orphans, the Trustees contested his exclusive authority over the orphanage by granting the local magistrates the right to oversee and intervene in all the institution's affairs. Their interference galled Whitefield, but in his extended absences, there was little he could do to prevent it. Whatever the lesson he taught about equality before God, the Trustees prevailed upon colonial officials to counter that message with a display of imperial power.[50]

And in South Carolina, evidence of the ultimate danger of Whitefield's message came in early 1742. Oglethorpe worried that Whitefield "had done much mischief in the colony," and it turned out that mischief had spread across the border. Hugh Bryan had been converting his own slaves and those on other plantations, allowing them to gather for worship. But he went further. Bryan sent prophecies to the South Carolina Assembly, predicting that unless southern society was reborn, "Charles Town . . . should be destroyed by fire and sword, to be executed by the Negroes." Immediately the Assembly ordered the arrest of Bryan and his "Abettors and Accomplices" in what sounded ominously like a conspiracy. Was Bryan sharing this revelation with the slaves, justifying mass revolt? Would it be a self-fulfilling prophesy? Evangelism seemed to beckon the most serious social disorder.[51]

South Carolina's planters closed ranks to deliver the strongest of messages to one of their own and indicted Bryan. Threatened with not merely complete ostracism, but prosecution and jail, he quickly repented; in a statement to the Assembly, published in the newspaper, he apologized for "the Disquiet I may have occasioned to my Country." He would continue to convert slaves to Christianity, but without the liberation theology component. As Alan Gallay puts it, "evangelicals were forced to accommodate to the political exigencies of a slaveholding society." The pressing danger had passed, but as far as elites were concerned, the Great Awakening should not be allowed to make real inroads into the Lower South.[52]

While Charles Town elites dealt with Bryan, they also dispatched Thomas Stephens back to London to reinvigorate the campaign for slavery. Stephens always claimed to represent the entire population of Georgia.[53] The Salzburgers argued "against such people and their Endeavors who presume and style themselves Agents of the People in Georgia; We have nothing to do with them and their selfinterested dangerous Contrivances," but their protests found no audience outside the Trustees. Even the tradesmen who had signed a petition in the desperate times of 1738 did not put their names to Stephens's documents.[54] But Stephens managed to convince enough parliamentarians of a crisis that, in May and June 1742, Parliament finally held hearings on Georgia. The Malcontents' lobbyist and witnesses urged Parliament not to approve any more public revenue for the colony, so that it would fail and the Trustees would abandon their plan. In a victory for the Trustees, the House rejected Stephens's attempts and punished him for libeling the Trustees, forcing him to receive a public rebuke on his knees. But the victory was bittersweet for Egmont, who heard later that the following day, Stephens was "impudently standing in the Lobby and with a gay countenance." Egmont tired of the struggle. As his health and energy waned, his attendance at the Board meetings declined.[55]

He was run into Debt more than he was able to pay, and that he knew not what Course to take; that he would go into the Army, and carry a Musquet.
—Defoe, *Moll Flanders*

Oglethorpe ran his military operation separately from the Trustees, and through 1741 and 1742, his preoccupation with St. Augustine led to infrequent communication with Savannah, let alone Egmont. The general dealt more with Indians in the Southeast and imperial military offices in London. No full engagements with the Spaniards occupied the community at Frederica, but allied Yamasee and Creek warriors raided and counter-raided during the spring of 1741, and at the end of the year, Oglethorpe unsuccessfully attempted another naval assault. Storms thwarted his plans.[56]

The role played by Indians in such colonial engagements was crucial, verified by analysis of Oglethorpe's expenditures. The British spent more on pay for the Creeks, the Cherokees, and the Choctaws than for their own regulars.[57] The accounts also reveal that local settlers who had emptied Savannah had not run away from the colony to find employment in South Carolina, as the Malcontents claimed. They had gone southward instead. Many assisted the regiment in such roles as piloting and crewing vessels of all kinds along the rivers and coastal waterways and also in well-paid tasks such as "tailoring Indians uniforms." Like local Indians, civilian settlers scored a significant payday in the war years, including the years between major engagements from the summer of 1740 until the summer of 1742. Money from the British military coffers flowed freely. Stories of Georgia's death were greatly exaggerated.[58]

Throughout the spring of 1742, the Spanish prepared to take back Georgia. Ten ships from Cuba sailed to St. Augustine in support. Oglethorpe spent those months feverishly erecting defenses around St. Simon's Island, anticipating a major offensive. He was not mistaken. Almost 2,000 men on board a fleet of over fifty vessels left Augustine for the retaking of Georgia on June 20. Highlanders in Darien evacuated women and children, including the widows and orphans of the Fort Mosa debacle, and rushed to Frederica with vengeance on their minds. Despite Oglethorpe's efforts to blockade, the Spanish made landfall on St. Simon's on July 6. The only hope for the much smaller British force lay in surprise. Led by Chickasaws and Creeks, some of the Highlanders attacked in the woods before the Spaniards could be organized into traditional lines of battle. Reeling, the Spanish general tried to regroup and sent grenadiers to hold Oglethorpe's force in check. These troops walked into another ambush, and at the Battle of Bloody Marsh, Highland men drove off the Spaniards and recovered their morale and their reputation. It was the last substantial fight from St. Augustine.[59]

The results of that action saved the colony in one respect. St. John's River became accepted as the default boundary between Britain and Spain. Oglethorpe had won great prestige—he would be promoted to brigadier general as a result—but even as imperial goals had been met, an important factor in keeping Georgia free dissolved. Betty Wood describes the victory at Bloody Marsh as "an important nail in the coffin of the Trustees' social design." One of the original reasons for the prohibition of slavery in the new colony had been its proximity to Florida. The argument was that so long as the Spanish there offered freedom and then used the ex-slaves as soldiers against the British colonies, slaves in Georgia, so close to the frontier, might easily become warriors against the mother country. However, as the Spanish would gradually cease contesting for the region, helping slaves escape would sink lower on their priority list. The imperial security argument lost its power to persuade policy makers in London of the need to keep slavery illegal in Georgia.[60]

Just one week before the battle, Thomas Stephens laughed off the scolding of the Speaker of the House of Commons. One week after, the Trustees asked William Stephens to begin an investigation "whether . . . it is proper to admit the use and introduction of Negroes in the said Province." Egmont penned his letter of resignation from the Board of Trustees the following day. Carolina planters licked their lips and girded their loins to continue the fight to introduce the Atlantic slave trade to Savannah. The battle for Georgia's soul remained in doubt.[61]

5

CREDIT AND BLAME, 1742–1749

It was always agreeable to the Inhabitants to have Families come among them to Plant, who brought Substance with them, either to purchase Plantations, or begin New ones.
—Defoe, *Moll Flanders*

As the threat of Spanish invasion slowly receded, the civilian population had to cope with the typical postwar economic dislocation. The military action had caused enormous upheaval in a colony struggling to find its feet. Many settlers had temporarily fled to Charles Town, and upon return had to deal with lost harvests. Goods had become extraordinarily expensive, given the risks of shipping during wartime, but the employment opportunities for single men around Frederica drove up wages in Savannah. Poor whites had a momentary chance to get ahead. Yet the momentum began to swing in favor of those advocating for slavery, not so much because of the old Malcontents, but as a result of Egmont's departure from the Board of Trustees, Oglethorpe's departure from Georgia, and the dwindling energy and power of William Stephens. As commerce rather than agriculture began to drive the politics of Georgia over the next few years, James Habersham, the young prodigy of Whitefield, emerged as the most powerful man in Savannah. But the Methodist theology of the lowly did not become the governing ethos of Georgia. Unaware of Habersham's schemes, the young men at Frederica never organized to combat his plan to lock them out of social mobility.

The war did not end with Bloody Marsh, and Oglethorpe even planned another attempt to take Augustine. There would be no further action in Georgia, however. As news of the victory at Bloody Marsh reached Charles Town and the surrounding plantations, the Savannah settlers who had fled there trickled back home. Habersham led the orphans back to Bethesda from their refuge at Hugh Bryan's plantation. It was not a joyous homecoming for all the small farmers; some discovered huge damage inflicted upon their plantations, while others were immediately beset by the malarial fevers of the summer. Most young men remained at Frederica, serving in the forces or as support, as boatmen, for example. So throughout the next year, the colonial officials maintained the chant to London that servants were impossible to get, or impossible to motivate, and as for free laborers, "none at present to be found to do [work] at tollerable Wages."[1]

Fears of the Spanish heightened again in the fall, but Oglethorpe and the regiment in the southern portion of the colony successfully repelled another attack in October 1742. For the next few years, while Savannah languished, the area around Frederica and Darien hummed with life. Jobs in the military and in supportive roles kept men busy, earning good money and enjoying a more reliable supply of rum, according to William Stephens: "Most Boats Crews that come here, being addicted to it remarkably beyond all others." Stephens and his council witnessed little of the activity. They could see only that the port town seemed empty and that their own plantations produced scantily because they could not or would not do the heavy farming work or they could not find anyone to do it for the money they were willing to pay. Thus their reports to the Trustees reinforced the arguments of the Malcontents that white people could not succeed in Georgia without black slaves.[2]

Proving these assumptions groundless were the hundreds of Salzburgers producing thousands of bushels of corn, rice, peas, and potatoes, and some of the German servants who finished their terms at the end of 1742 and requested land grants at Acton and Vernonburgh. Thirty new lots were laid out on White Bluff for the ex-servants and more soon for erstwhile residents of Purrysburg, South Carolina. (Purrysburg had been founded around the same time as Georgia and attracted many German farmers. There, slavery was permitted, but in an object lesson for the small farmers of Georgia if they paid attention, those without sufficient capital to purchase very expensive slaves were no more going to grow rich quickly than the poor of London.) More ex-servants would make their way to Acton over the next year, while Purrysburg also sent people to Ebenezer. The settlers in the new communities went straight to work, stunning Stephens with the industry they had never shown when they had been under indenture. By January 1744, they had cleared a huge area and begun cultivating. Meanwhile other boosters prepared to lead new settlers from Virginia. None of these fresh arrivals enlarged Savannah, however; the population of the town remained in the low hundreds.[3]

Stephens and the Trustees failed to grasp that the class strictures limiting the autonomy of the working poor in England just did not apply in the colonies. The switch from a surplus of labor in London to a dearth of impoverished people to exploit in Savannah produced such an upside-down world that they could not adapt their expectations quickly enough.

The whining of the landed classes about the amount they had to pay people continued through the 1740s. Rather than accept the even relative flattening of the social and economic hierarchy to include a middling sort of well-paid artisans, they pushed for slavery. Exacerbated by the presence of the military, "a labouring man no sooner sets his foot but he can find good pay with little work, by entering in some Branch or other of the Military Service," planters objected to the market realities for wages. Like Mrs. Camuse, however, poor men adopted the stance of a person of value, instead of the "gratefull Obedience as a Servant" the higher-ups expected.[4]

Having secured an alliance with the Creeks, Oglethorpe planned another attack on St. Augustine in the spring of 1743. Moving to Amelia Island in March, from there Creek warriors launched a raid on the Spanish. They killed five and then headed home, having achieved their goals. As usual, Indian concepts of warfare and military glory did not align with the European perspective, leaving many of the latter group frustrated that the "savages" did not accept their ranked authority. But Oglethorpe did learn certain strategies from his allies. He had grasped the necessity of the surprise attack. Without further Creek assistance, the regiment headed to St. Augustine. Oglethorpe tried to trick the Spanish into leaving the Castillo and facing an ambush, but they would not fall for his feint. Then two of the British force made their way over to the Spanish, and with those desertions, all hope of maintaining secrecy and the element of surprise was lost. Oglethorpe retreated. Even his plan to land on a small island to slaughter Spanish cattle stocked there failed.[5]

■ With Egmont severely curtailing his role in London, the Board there minimized the time they spent attending to Georgia affairs. In May 1743, they made some important policy decisions. Annoyed at Oglethorpe for occasionally billing the Trust instead of the Ministry of War for his expenses, they cut him out of all civil government and appointed William Stephens as president over the entire colony. It mattered little; Oglethorpe left Georgia that summer, never to return. Other major decisions included an end to sending servants who would work specifically for the Trust—failed efforts on public works such as the garden had disillusioned them—no more bounties on corn, peas, and potatoes, and instructions to keep a careful watch over the children at Bethesda. If they "are taught only Latin and . . . kept ignorant and unemploy'd in Business and Work, which their Stations in Life will make necessary for them to be instructed in and used to," the magistrates had the power to pull them out of the orphanage.

With fewer meetings over the rest of the year and in the years to follow, Stephens was left with a lot of power, but almost no money, "Cash being now run almost to the last Gasp." Parliament's grant in the spring of 1743 sufficed only to pay the arrears. The Trustees did not even petition for more funding until 1746. Few of them cared enough about the project to inject much energy. Oglethorpe enjoyed praise and celebrity back in London, and the romantic attentions of a lady with huge tracts of land. Fully reimbursed for his personal military expenses, he lobbied for further funding for the regiment, now under the command of Captain William Horton. But he never put any more effort into the philanthropic or philosophical ideal of a free-labor colony.[6]

There was money in Georgia all right, but little of it was in the hands of the ostensible government. While Stephens maintained a flow of begging letters to London over the mid-1740s, a canny young businessman with a little experience in the Atlantic commercial world saw an opportunity to cash in on the realm of government contracts. James Habersham, almost abandoned by Whitefield, whose fund-raising flagged as the Awakening subsided, had been trying to make Bethesda self-sufficient. Habersham had come to Georgia with Whitefield, having worked for several years as an apprentice of sorts to various merchants in London. As his biographer explains, "the City of London was unrivaled as a school of commerce." He spent the bulk of his time managing two sugar refineries and dealing with imports from the West Indies, and so grew familiar with the Atlantic trade. That trade required skills of relationship building and communication, in addition to understanding credit operations and risk management. All of these Habersham put into play in the mid-1740s in Savannah.[7]

Experimenting with a shipload of goods in 1741, of which profits were intended to benefit the orphanage, Habersham learned what would sell and what would not in the colony. Over the next few years, he cornered the Georgia market. In partnership with Francis Harris, he dealt with the army officers who sent for provisions, willing to pay military rates, but he also cleverly extended credit to the colonial officials around Savannah. He could wait for their salaries eventually to appear from London, and in the meantime, Stephens and the assistants grew completely dependent upon his goodwill, as they noted they had been "entirely Supported on the Credit of the Estimate by Retailers of Stores." By the summer of 1744, Habersham and Harris were setting up shop on the best lots for the purpose in Savannah. At an astonishing pace, they roped in over 50 percent of the public budget. Jonathan Barber, the religious leader at Bethesda in

Whitefield's absence, took over the management of the children, although Habersham claimed at least at first that the orphanage provided the motivation for his business affairs.[8]

In the absence of Oglethorpe and Whitefield, William Stephens should have been the unquestioned leader of the colony through the mid-1740s, but that was not the case. While Habersham's power of the purse kept Savannah's administrators beholden, the Augusta settlement had never paid much heed to decrees emanating from either London or Savannah anyhow and gradually South Carolinians felt secure enough to slip slaves over the line in that region. Meanwhile, in Frederica, Captain Horton ruled the community. Civil authority supposedly rested in the hands of appointees Register John Terry and Magistrate John Calwell, but as Terry futilely complained to the Trustees, Horton "appropriates to him self here the Authority of a Prince (Nay Even that of Lewis the 14th)." The analogy of the Sun King certainly strains our credulity, but as most of the community worked in some capacity for the military, and therefore depended upon Horton's goodwill for their pay, it should not surprise us that his orders carried more weight than lowly colonial officials, "Empty Vessells . . . Tittles but No Power," as observers scoffed.[9]

The issue was not merely a question of petty officials jealous of encroachments on their jurisdictions. The power of the military commander comes through clearly in an awful incident in 1744. Terry described a brutal rape by an ensign, perpetrated with serious violence on a woman while others waited just outside the room. "He stopt her Mouth with his hankerchief And finding she Resisted him, he Continued Cutting her with the Horse whip." The bleeding woman finally submitted and afterward the soldier "hinted to her . . . he had Given her the french Disease." Escaping through the window while the other soldiers debated who should go next, the victim ran to Horton and then to Calwell, the civil magistrate. Her wounds clearly visible, and the crime so outrageous, Calwell told her he needed input from Terry. But by the time Terry arrived for the hearing the next day, Horton had purchased the woman's silence to protect his men from jail. She showed Terry and Calwell the "£10 she had rec'd As a Recompence for what had Happned, And was Made to give them what she call'd a Bond Never to Prosecute None of them."[10]

Terry and Calwell would describe other attempted assaults, including a case where the accused soldier's defence was that "the young Woman had Invited him to Her bed," which the military court accepted "as The Gospel." Terry believed in the virtue of the young woman, who now "had Infamy & shame for her Innosence." Along with Calwell, he also charged

Horton with covering up many kinds of lesser malfeasances in courts martial, cases that should have been tried in civil court. But the rape story, told so vividly, reminds us not merely of the horrors of war and the preciousness of an impartial justice system. Eighteenth-century "gentlemen" held patriarchal ideas about gender roles and sexuality. One man in Frederica, found guilty of sodomy, was executed. Rape was acknowledged as a great crime, when a stranger was the perpetrator. But even when the villain received proper punishment, the act lessened the value of a woman, perhaps forever in her community. Loyalty to one's brethren, especially in the military whose values included esprit de corps, trumped care for women, who after all, were inferior creatures, akin to beloved pets over whom men exercised full power, and who owed devotion to their protectors. One should not mistreat them, yet men hesitated to interfere or pass judgment when their peers were abusive.[11]

In the particular circumstances of 1740s Frederica, Horton and his successor, Alexander Heron, abused their power by stretching it beyond their appointed measure. Perhaps they told themselves they had to; the community certainly seemed like an extension of the regiment, and with attention from London waning and Stephens's health prohibiting much travel for him, they could argue that they were the obvious center of authority. The discipline necessary to conduct warfare in this period, requiring men to march toward enemy cannon, placed extraordinary power in the hands of commanding officers, however, and when such commanders expanded their jurisdictions into civil matters, a cauldron of corruption began to brew. Terry's punishment for daring to challenge Horton's authority was to find himself charged with rape "on the Body of his Servant Maid," but when the case came to court, the woman in question denied Terry had assaulted her and said her husband had "forced her to make two false Oaths."[12]

Everyday life in the colony in the mid-1740s felt good to the young man working for the British army in southern Georgia. Most reenlisted when their first term of service expired. The risk of warfare receded, and the biggest concern might have been sanitation, given the hot climate and few women to demand or perhaps incentivize basic hygiene. However, a local chemist claimed he had concocted a potion from the native plants that cured malaria, "Ague & Feavor & all other Feavors," and the very same prescription apparently even managed to treat both gout and "the small Pox without Pitts" (without leaving scars). The medicine would induce a "Great Sweat" and the amazing results confounded the doctors. This forerunner to our pharmaceutical companies pushed his drug especially for "sailers and soulders," as their notorious mortality rates might draw a great deal of business his way.[13]

Georgia heat remained formidable to Englishmen, and the summer months must have accentuated the stench wafting from the men and their cramped housing. Six men shared each twelve-by-fourteen-foot hut. Sweat, decaying teeth, flatulence, latrines: a lethal combination to the human nose and yet so attractive to flies. Add horses to the malodorous mix and picture how swarming bugs found their version of paradise in Frederica. But young men in the colonial era tolerated scents we can only imagine in our nightmares, and so they may have considered their moist friends' stinking body odor a welcoming aura as they came home from a day's hunt spent among snakes and alligators. The reek from the latrine area signaled human companionship, and the lads with the rotten breath laughed as lads do now, at buddies who suffered toilet troubles and their never-laundered pants.[14]

They worked at a less than hectic pace—patrolling waned as the Spanish threat diminished—and leisure hours allowed them to explore the region. Once adjusted to the heat and the insect multitudes, some harbored hopes of carving out a home in this foreign wilderness, where a man who had no prospects in England could start a farm or a craftsman's shop and become his own boss. He would need a wife, of course; Oglethorpe had written letters imploring the Trustees to send young women, and they in more promising times had indicated they hoped "to send also Women over for Wives." A farm household was at least a two-person job. If women could be recruited, the possibility of true economic freedom existed for poor white people in Georgia in the Trustee era, and these soldiers, in all their gloriously eye-watering filth, represented the promise of a colony of free people.[15]

In place of marriageable-aged women, all the Trustees could send were casks and casks of . . . shoes. In a perfect example of their ignorance of the situation on the ground, the Board felt it was in the best interests of Georgian settlers to receive several large shipments of footwear, that it might serve as a "usefull Specie," or a type of currency. To the bewilderment of Stephens in Savannah, the first two casks, received in the summer of 1743, were followed by four more in early 1744 and another shipment the next year. All this while government officials had zero cash to pay themselves or meet any of the colony's bills. Stephens assured them this was a fruitless endeavor; several servants had become shoemakers upon the finish of their indentures "& sell cheaper than English Shoes can be afforded at," but his words fell on deaf ears. To add insult to injury, the

1745 cargo, poorly packed for Atlantic travel, was "decayed & perishing long before they came out of England."[16]

■ Thomas Stephens's campaign continued for a little while longer. He was back in the South in the late spring of 1743, trying to round up financial backers, to continue his posture as "agent" of the settlers. (Some believed that William Stephens himself was now convinced by his son, others that the Trustees ordered the elderly Stephens to "write nothing butt good Accounts of the Colony.") While Thomas began to change some minds, not too many felt sufficiently flush to hire him. The debate circulated without consensus within the colony. Further afield, however, only one message was received: Georgia was dying. The planters of Charles Town with their extensive Atlantic networks, painted a picture of a failed colony. Almost everyone from Boston to Jamaica to London believed that potential immigrants needed to look to Pennsylvania or North Carolina, for white men could not succeed in Georgia. The whispering campaign had reached distant shores, and Thomas Stephens moved out of the picture. Habersham picked up the baton and carried it over the finishing line.[17]

Habersham envisioned a colony, full of workers and their children enslaved in perpetuity, topped by a few, powerful gentlemen whose status knew no upper boundary, at least on this side of the Atlantic. Fed by the example of Charles Town and its magnificence, soaring pride and the temptation of significance captured another in its clutches. Despite the exhortations to humility Whitefield delivered in every sermon, his most devoted follower completed the machinations that would finally bring slavery to Savannah and wealth into his own coffers.

Records do not show how or when Habersham made his peace with a Methodist God on the subject of material accumulation, but perhaps his time at the Bryans' plantation helped him philosophize a reconciliation between slavery and the lowly Christ. We can only tell that in the fall of 1744, William Stephens reported that Habersham scarcely mentioned Whitefield any more. In the meantime, Rev. Bolzius felt increasing pressure to silence himself on the topic of the day. Stephens's health and lack of government funds began to hinder his ability to control the other magistrates, Henry Parker and Charles Watson, who did not disguise their cooperation with his son the pro-slavery lobbyist. They refused to help Bolzius in the minor administrative ways Stephens always had, recognizing that when the Salzburgers successfully modeled a free-labor economy, it damaged their claims for the necessity of African slaves. Bolzius's complaints to that effect were corroborated by the schoolmaster Dobell, who told the Trustees that any gesture of support they offered Bolzius "like a Bone of fish it sticks in the Maws of your back-handed friends." Dobell suspected Stephens was "sliping through his Lordships and your Honours Hands as Water does," worn down by the fatigue of defending a system after the principal exponents had deserted. Without regular and hearty endorsements from Egmont and Oglethorpe, Stephens gradually surrendered the fight.[18]

Another official helped illuminate the passage of power from Stephens through Parker and Watson to Habersham. Patrick Graham, charged by the Trustees with the formidable task of making sense of Georgia's account books, explained that the sola bills (official government currency) were delayed by accidents at sea during the war, causing the colony's business to fall in arrears. Habersham and Harris took advantage by extending credit, but then stockpiling the bills once they did arrive, thus developing further the magistrates' dependence on them. Generous with grants of credit to government officers, Habersham built allegiances and indebtedness as political weapons and was prepared to use them when he saw fit. The debts of the officials rendered them vulnerable. When Habersham needed their cooperation, he could threaten to enforce payment by seizing their goods or some equally humiliating show.[19]

I took especial care to buy for him all those things I knew he
delighted to have; as two good long Wigs, two silver hilted Swords,
three or four fine Fowling pieces, a fine Saddle with Holsters and
Pistoles very handsome, with a Scarlet Cloak; and in a Word, every
thing I could think of to oblige him; and to make him appear,
as he really was, a very fine Gentleman.
—Defoe, *Moll Flanders*

In Virginia, such accoutrements marked a planter. And even in early Savannah one government officer, Charles Watson, hankered after the finer things in life. Habersham catered to his whims, beyond his means to pay. "Addicted to the Study & Practice of . . . how to appear Gay, & outshine all about him in vain & costly Apparel" from the warehouse of Habersham and Harris, Watson fell deeper in debt. He was not the only man to do so. Workers of all stripes and strata shopped at the store, turning over their pay packet to Habersham when cash of any kind finally appeared. William Stephens felt no sympathy for the laborer, whatever the level of interest paid; "Wages being grown so exorbitant, that Day Labourers were in a manner become our Masters." Elites found it outrageous that the poor might want to pursue a measure of economic success beyond that deemed acceptable for them by their betters. Elizabethan sumptuary laws may never have been effectively enforced, but the underlying concept, that people adhere to the rank they were born, died hard among the upper crust.[20]

That concept of lineage determining the limits of the economic possible is anathema to Americans, but the revolutionary creation of a nation founded on the premise of equality of opportunity was three decades away. The official challenge to the concept of rank by birth came with a Declaration by the colonies in 1776, but the idea had been building for a long time among the European settlers in the New World. Whitefield spent more time in the North, but egalitarian ideas continued to permeate Georgia. "If you Ask any Man you Meet in the Street, how he came to Swear, Get Drunk &c he'll Answer with an Oath, have not I the same Libtie as my Rulers have." When organizing guard duty in Savannah during the war, Stephens was forced by the populace to include everyone in rotation, for they would permit "no distinction of persons, but every one from the Highest to the lowest, was bound to appear every Seventh night, which gave great Contentment among the people." All this, as the "uncommon Brevity" of the Trustees' letters to Stephens left him floundering in Savannah.[21]

The moral, rather than economic, debate on the issue of slavery crescendoed at the end of 1745 when the two dominant religious leaders of the colony clarified their teaching on the matter. On Christmas Eve, Bolzius composed a long missive to Whitefield, who had recently come back to visit Bethesda. He appointed a new manager, and spent time with Habersham, "relishing only the Company of the greatest," as one erstwhile devotee described. At this point, Whitefield decisively came down on the pro-slavery side and petitioned the Trustees to allow the introduction of enslaved workers, probably at the behest of Habersham, for he claimed that Bethesda orphanage required a slave-based plantation to remain above water. In any case, Bolzius took apart the arguments one by one, albeit on a different moral basis than modern antiracists might stand.[22]

The commonality of outlook between the two pastors was a firm commitment to the message of a lowly Christ who loved the white Christian poor. From that perspective, each man answered the question how best the poor white man could be served in Georgia. Whitefield held that the introduction of slavery would make the larger colonial economy thrive, creating unspecified opportunities for everyone. Bolzius pointed out that whatever gains the economy made would not necessarily improve the lot of all. Referencing South Carolina multiple times as the model, he described the process of capital accumulation in the hands of a few.

> A Common white Labourer in Charles Town (I am told) has no more Wages, than a Negroe for his work . . . for which it is in my Opinion impossible to find Victuals, Lodging & washing, much Less Cloaths. In case he would Settle & Cultivate a plantation, is not all good & Convenient Ground at the Sea Coasts & Banks of the Rivers taken up in Large Quantities by the Merchants & Other Gentlemen? Consequently the poor white Inhabitants are forced to possess Lands, remote from the Conveniency of Rivers & from Town to their great Disappointment to Sell their produce. Then they are discouraged & Oblidged to Seek their Livelihood in the Garrisons, Forts, Scout-Boats, Trading Boats or to be imploy'd amongst the Negroes upon a Gentleman's Plantation, or they are forced to take Negroes upon Credit, of which they will find in Process of time the Sad Consequences on Account of their Debts.[23]

With so little industry providing employment in the colonial South, few jobs, and none well paid, remained for the majority of white workers, once employers had the possibility of not paying wages at all. The independent life of the yeoman farmer, however, could only be a dream while the great planters swallowed up the best lands, a process Bolzius correctly prophesized.

As for the premise pushed by the Malcontents from the beginning and now picked up by Whitefield, that the southern climate precluded pasty cold-blooded Europeans from functioning in the fields, Bolzius went further than merely presenting the Salzburger community as refutation. He discussed a variety of strategies farmers might adopt in Georgia to avoid hoeing in the height of a Savannah midsummer afternoon. "Have they not 9 Months in the Year time Enough to prepare the Ground for Europian & Countrey Grain?" Certainly, horses or oxen to pull a plough solved the problem entirely. And the early failures resulted from poor understanding of how best to exploit the land. Bolzius explained it had taken time for him to learn the lumber business, for example, but now a great chance lay to attract the Germans currently flooding Pennsylvania. He called out Whitefield on his true loyalties: "It is a Thousand pity, that you will help to make this Retirement & Refuge for poor persecuted or Necessitous Protestants, a Harbour of Black Slaves."[24]

Pennsylvania's population exploded in the first half of the eighteenth century, and while enslaved Africans contributed to the economic development of the colony, they primarily worked in Philadelphia, not in agriculture. Indentured servants from Britain and the German princi-palities constituted the majority of the labor pool; upon their hard work, a prosperous society grew while nurturing a distinctive egalitarian ethos. As Bolzius argued, there existed no reason that the same model could not function in Georgia. The crux lay in the consciences of those with choices: the men of capital. "Mr. Habersham had hitherto no black Slaves, Not-withstanding he advanced very well in his trade . . . I hope he has reason to thank the Lord for it. . . . I wish the Gentlemen would employ their good parts & Money not only for their Own Self Interest, but make it Likewise their Business, to help the poor honest white Labourers upon their Legs, which easily they could do by buying their Lumber, & sending it to West India, they would Serve themselves, & have the Blessing of God, who loves the poor despised people."[25]

The pastor saved his fiercest punch for last. In this battle between Christian leaders, the decisive victory would go to the man who could save the most souls. Whitefield claimed that with slavery, he could lead the hea-thens of Africa to Christ. Bolzius pointed out that in the very act of doing do, Whitefield would condemn the souls of white farmers. "As long as they are for this World, & take Advantage of the Poor Black Slaves, they will increase the Sins of the Land to a great Heighth." He picked apart the holes in Whitefield's argument. Few sought to save the souls of those already enslaved in the New World and little of Whitefield's energies over the seven previous years had been directed to that end. "If a Minister had a Call to imploy his Strength & time to Convert Negroes, he has in Carolina a Large Field."[26]

Knowing that the war with Spain had helped some Trustees defend the slavery ban—slaves would run to the Florida boundary, grasp freedom, and immediately fight the British in Georgia—Bolzius declared that God intended the war purposefully, to proscribe slavery. He finished with a re-ligious flourish, threatening Whitefield with the wrath of the Almighty should he not change course. "I beg the Lord for you, not to lead you into that Temptation to Contribute any thing to the Overthrow of the Trust-ees's good Schemes, & to fill the Colony with Negroes, for which you hardly will reap a Blessing from the Hand of God here and hereafter." But about a year later, a Whitefield supporter purchased a slave-worked plantation in Carolina, the proceeds of which would benefit the orphanage.[27]

Bolzius's plea for the soul of Georgia only marked him as a spoiler in the eyes of the powerful. His case, intertwining careful observations over many years in the region and heartfelt spiritual faith, was much tighter than that of the various Malcontents. Why could Georgia not build an economy and society on the Pennsylvania model, rather than on South Carolina's? Others around the colony agreed with such a possibility. But the few great planters of Carolina wanted otherwise and relentlessly pursued every avenue toward their vision. The Protestant South placated its conscience for the next century with the notion that because coming to the New World apparently saved the souls of Africans, they could justify the Atlantic slave trade, the domestic slave trade, the selling of people on auction blocks, and all the rest of the constant brutal violence on which the American Gulag depended.[28]

During the spring of 1746, Habersham tried to create a unanimous voice among the colonial officials by visiting any dissenters from the proslavery line and attempting to persuade them of "the hardships of Georgia under the Trustees Administration." Revealing his sense of his growing importance, Habersham claimed he could get a post on the Council whenever he desired. But with William Stephens still trying to hold the Trustee line on slavery and Bolzius standing tall as an example of the potential of a free Georgia, the storekeeper decided to choose a different tack than the overtly political.[29]

That summer, Habersham consulted with planters in South Carolina and figured out a scheme he hoped would soon force the hands of the Trustees and Parliament into lifting the slavery ban. Whether from a lack of attention on the part of the Board or Atlantic hostilities, again the colonial officials found themselves cash-strapped and "driven to the Necessity of seeking Credit . . . Harris and Habersham have been the principal Dealers who have given those Credits." Suddenly in June, the storekeepers announced a complete credit freeze, even for official government business, fomenting "an universal Distraction among all Ranks of People in this part of the Colony." Stephens and a couple of the other officials smelt a rat. They knew Habersham had just returned from Charles Town and felt "the Scheme taking Effect" had been "moulded" there. The goal was to create such financial distress as to provoke "an Insurrection." With Trustee government proven entirely incompetent, Habersham could step up as the man who could salvage the solvency of the colony, provided he got what he wanted. This move enraged some of the officials, who knew that Habersham's fast riches had come from government contracts over the previous years. To thwart this plan, Graham agreed to leave immediately for South Carolina to procure bread and rice. The response worked; credit reopened, but remained "precarious" for the rest of the year, as Habersham flexed his muscles and awaited his moment. Stephens realized the strategy: "It is the most effectual Way to bring the Colony to Destruction," but he found no major solution. The debtors included, after all, the Board of Trustees. Habersham's strident demands for payment for government arrears from a Board that requested less than £10,000 from Parliament between 1743 and 1750 surely made conceding to his pressure for slavery easier.[30]

After a decade of the Trustees doggedly trying to encourage agricultural settlement, requests for large tracts of land suddenly poured into the Council over the course of 1747 and continued in years to follow. Confidence spread through Charles Town that the hated prohibition of slavery neared an end, and the time had come to lay claim to the richest lands to the south. Other small farm families also steadily pushed their way into unoccupied areas, down the Great Wagon road that led settlers into the backcountry of North Carolina and South Carolina during the 1740s. The Georgia Council determined who deserved acreage, however. And in allotting lands, they favored already substantial planters. Men considered "well to pass in the World and capable of cultivating such a Tract" received many hundreds of acres at a time, despite the constant moan about a labor shortage in Georgia. In contrast, ex-apprentices and servants out of their time were awarded fifty-acre lots. Occasionally in the Council minutes, a strangely conflicting discussion is recorded, such as in the early months of 1748. The Council, apparently shocked to hear that some of the South Carolinian recipients of their largesse had moved slaves onto the lands granted them, declared they intend to reject requests "of the like Nature from the Inhabitants of South Carolina: We being fully convinced that their general Design is to introduce and use their Negroes."[31]

The explanation came a few years later. William Stephens's health declined steadily, in no small part as a result of the enormous stress of running a colony with no money and the persistent opposition of a group "whose Motto seemeth to me to be 'Let's weary them in their own devices.'" Stephens undoubtedly felt weary, and he gradually stepped back from government while the other magistrates wrote the letters and reports back to London. Perhaps in a spell of good health in early 1748, he demanded to know why so many South Carolinians escaped punishment for flagrant lawbreaking. The rest of the assistants on the Council placated him, blaming the state of affairs on Heron and supporting in print his declarations. They would explain to the Trustees later that Stephens's mind was "confused; and altho' his Name has always appear'd at the Head of the Board, yet for some time past, he has been utterly uncapable of any Business, but rather retarded it." All seemed to be moving, even if in fits and starts, toward Habersham's goal.[32]

As Habersham turned the credit screw, others launched a hate campaign against Bolzius who, merely by persevering, exposed the falsehoods at the center of the Malcontent crusade. As the credit crunch bit, the first reports of vicious gossip aimed at the pastor emerged. Despite pleas from other Ebenezer farmers to continue protesting, because they feared that slavery would set them back economically, Bolzius had to consider his personal security. "'Tis almost incredible to belive what ill blood and base underhanded Opposition is for this Cause continually fomenting and carrying on against him . . . to weaken his Hands and blacken his Character," reported one Savannah resident. As 1747 passed, the malicious talk intensified, and not only within Georgia. Those traveling through Charles Town were also subject to rants against Bolzius. "The jealousy & rage of English, French & Dutch people is so much kindled against me," that he believed "my life in danger" and begged the Trustees not to mention his name in any letters to the Georgia Council. He tendered his resignation as manager of all civil affairs at Ebenezer. A few days later, he penned another letter, surrendering at last the fight against slavery. Frightened by the death threats, Bolzius had grasped "the blame will be at last intirely upon me." Citing his position as a foreigner, he thought he should not be "obstructive" and stepped back from the fray and instead immersed himself in a new health problem besetting Ebenezer.[33]

■ The moment of truth for Georgia occurred when Colonel Alexander Heron arrived in Frederica to demobilize the regiment.[34] Not for another year would diplomats sign the peace at Aix-la-Chapelle, but for the Georgia colony, life abruptly changed in the fall of 1747. Four years after their last mission, the soldiers and the support network around them heard their part in King George's War was officially over. The extended tension with the Spanish that had shifted the attention of Oglethorpe from civil affairs, had destroyed several harvests as security concerns insisted settlers run to Charles Town or enlist in the army, had interrupted communication with England, had left Savannah deserted as Frederica hummed, and had so wreaked havoc on the original designs for the settlement suddenly ended. On one hand, the pro-slavery element thrilled that one more quiver in their opponents' arsenal had dropped. Spain could not use escaped slaves to attack Georgia. But on the other, a crop of young men acclimatized to the South and familiar by now with the terrain, the crops, and the farming techniques might morph into hardy yeoman farmers or, at least in the short term, into agricultural laborers. "Maybe it will be easier from now on to find fieldhands for hire," hoped Bolzius. Could the regiment bring to life the Trustees' vision?[35]

The disbanding of the regiment involved a long process, which included Heron's fairly immediate departure for Charles Town to gather provisions and clarify jurisdictional disagreements. And in the meantime, South Carolina planters, assured that only the war had postponed the inevitable, started to move their slaves south onto lands along the rivers and creeks. Many suggested that clandestinely, such activity had long passed without consequence around Augusta, close to the Carolina line. Now, as confidence soared that Stephens and Bolzius had been effectively silenced, slaves were spotted in Savannah and around the neighboring region. Throughout the fall and into 1748, the Council maintained to the Trustees that they used all their powers to prevent or to prosecute such shenanigans, insinuating that the regimental officers welcomed the slave owners into the Frederica area. Colonel Heron disputed their account as a ruse, accusing the magistrates of raising their glasses frequently to the toast "The One Thing Needful." Now even Stephens put his name to a letter that advised the Board lift the ban, lest all settlement cease.[36]

Many elements needed to turn Georgia into a southern Pennsylvania coalesced just as Habersham and the Charles Town elite shut that door. A few lone voices argued that Georgia's prospects for attracting farm families remained good. A number of soldiers (151) from the regiments and their families decided to stay. But by now Habersham called the shots. Even the ex-servants who had proved themselves "industrious" or a Pennsylvanian farmer who brought "a numerous growing Family and he himself appearing a hail lusty laborious Man" would win at most 200 acres, whereas South Carolinians might receive 500 acres for the father and each son. If the Council deemed an applicant "not of great Substance" or "of no great Circumstances," their allotment was a fraction of that given to the already wealthy. One last petition to the Trustees begged for some attention to the needs of small farmers: "We fear the Gentlemen of the Councill will not have Such Regard to us as we might expect from them they being taken up much with Great 500 acre Gentlemen." But it was too little, too late.[37]

The Board of Trustees surrendered in August 1748. They penned a letter to the Georgia Council explaining that slavery would be permitted with some limitations by the following year and asking the president and assistants to gather community leaders for a discussion on those limits, such as the precise ratio of black to white they thought advisable. As this news reached Georgians, "even the poorest and lowest people" celebrated. Bolzius wryly pondered "whether the poor in this country will benefit as much from the import of Negroes as they believe." But he did not voice such skepticism aloud in Savannah.[38]

Early in 1749, the Council and others such as Bolzius and Habersham completed the task, suggesting a ratio that did not take into account the numbers of slave children that might be born. They agreed that all slaves should be prevented from learning or practicing any trades except coopering and sawyering, essential skills on a plantation. Slaves should be guaranteed Sundays off, and any cruel "Proprietor of Negroes" subject to trial and punishment no different than for abuse of a white person. Anyone who had spent a few days in Charles Town understood how absurd these provisions read, but if it salved the guilt of the London Board enough to secure an end to the prohibition, then they would play along.[39]

Rumors flew for a brief spell that Georgia would be annexed to South Carolina, understandably, because in effect planters like Jonathan Bryan would soon be moving south and extending the rice economy. Perhaps the Charles Town planters debated such a development. Bolzius, particularly worried what this would mean for his Salzburgers, was greatly relieved to find it untrue. Habersham and a few other Savannah locals feared losing their clout. He became a public official in the spring of 1749, completing his passage to power.[40]

Habersham's debtors had been pressured, bribed, and convinced to use their influence to open the port of Savannah to the slave trade, a trade that would take him from the ranks of the wealthy (by Trustee Savannah standards) to "an income that would have placed him comfortably among England's landed gentry." His win reminds us of all the possibilities of colonial America: an orphan boy with a mix of hardscrabble pluck and smarts, apprenticed in London in his teens, makes good in the New World and climbs to the top of the ladder. That victory over an entrenched British class system might lead us to cheer, if it had only happened in any other way. But it happened because of a substitution in hierarchical systems: race surpassed class as the binding identity, cutting off ambition for some while justifying another's success at the expense of a "lesser" person. We might not demand that James Habersham overthrow white supremacy, even in his own brain; too few individuals within his world proved capable of that level of critical thinking. Two generations of white southerners had been immersed in the "common sense" that skin tone accurately indicated intelligence, beauty, and human value before Habersham stepped off the boat. Nor can we sit in religious judgment: Moravians and Salzburgers and Quakers around the colonies enslaved others, and the Bible is a flexible text. But for a man from his class background, exposed to (supposedly devoted to) the idea of a God who washed the feet of others, can twenty-first-century historians ask even this question: that he seek equality of opportunity for those of his own tribe? Instead, the plantation society he fathered in Georgia cut off the level playing field.[41]

6

DEFEAT, 1750s

He sent me a Maid-Servant, and a Negro Boy to wait on me,
and Provisions ready dress'd for my Supper; and thus I was as if
I had been in a new World.
—Defoe, *Moll Flanders*

Moll Flanders enjoyed a life of luxury in the American South. Early in adulthood, she had traveled to Virginia with her second husband and bore him a son. In a plot twist not unlike that of modern soap operas, she learned to her enormous shock that her husband was her biological half brother. Fleeing the scene, Moll spent most of her adult life back in England, marrying frequently, and eventually settling into the life of a pickpocket. Several decades later, the state transported her back to Virginia for her crimes. In an amazing coincidence, she immediately encountered the son she had abandoned, now living as a successful Virginia planter. He warmly welcomed his mother, setting Moll and her latest spouse up for life on a beautiful Chesapeake plantation. Accustomed to the massive inequities of England, she adjusted quickly from a society that based its rigid hierarchy on lineage to one built on race. Although born in Newgate, at the very bottom of the English social scale, Moll was now waited on by the lowest rank in the colonies, the African slave. As readers, we are tempted to cheer for Moll the charming rascal, so entertainingly uninhibited by the bourgeois moral code. But Defoe neglected any description of the life of that "Negro Boy." And if Defoe's English readers believed that Moll's rags-to-riches story awaited any white person who settled the southern colonies, they succumbed to fantasy.

As the 1740s turned into the 1750s, Georgia transformed from a Trust colony at war, aimed at providing opportunities for poor white people, into a Royal colony at peace, providing opportunities to a select few. The switch included a period without governance from England at all, and into that breach stepped a couple of Whitefield devotees, James Habersham and Jonathan Bryan. Nervous at first about what the change would mean, gradually they took advantage of the power vacuum until the arrival of the first Royal governor in 1754 and established a new Georgia in their own interests. If the meek hoped to inherit the earth, they would have to await the Second Coming.

■ The end of the war and demobilization of the regiment frightened a few Savannah residents, and not merely because of the threatening French, now building their chain of forts and trading posts encircling British settlements. Businessmen Habersham and Harris found themselves deprived of lucrative military contracts and worried about their bottom line. Could their merchant house survive without government expenditures? Habersham took his seat on the Board as the doddering William Stephens grew more tired, confused, and defeated.

Within months of the departure of most soldiers, word came from King Malatchee of the Lower Creeks that a large contingent of his people headed for Savannah. Mary Musgrove Bosomworth, foremost liaison between Indians and the British colonials since 1733, had apparently invited her kinsfolk to town to bring a little pressure to bear in support of her land claims. In the midst of the barrage of petitions for land in the wake of slavery, Bosomworth wanted assurance that the beautiful islands of St. Catherines, Sapelo, and Ossabaw belonged to her. The colonial officials most certainly did not want to honor what Bosomworth argued was a gift from Tomochichi, but the news of the Lower Creeks coming en masse did not fill their hearts with joy, either. The Board immediately sent emergency letters to London, begging for money for an interpreter and for a draft "in favour of Messrs Harris and Habersham for One Hundred Pounds to answer the Daily growing expences on this Occasion."[1]

Stephens, still acting president, assumed "some Secret and dangerous designs" by Bosomworth and hosted a dinner for Malatchee and other leaders to convince them of Georgia's friendship to all Creeks. But within a week, hundreds of Indians were in the vicinity "demanding large quantities of provisions." The Board's reports indicate that the officials assumed Bosomworth and her husband riled up their visitors. So they summoned a militia, while trying to come between Bosomworth and the rest of the Lower Creek leadership with diplomacy: these efforts were hampered, they claimed, by Indian drunkenness. Gradually over the month of August, a series of meetings saw them try to convince the Creeks that the Bosomworths only used them and actually schemed to take a hugely disproportionate amount of the presents dispatched by the British government for them all.[2]

After a few dramatic scenes related in the reports, the majority of the Creek delegation received the presents, felt "well Satisfied," and departed for home, to the great relief of most Savannah residents. "Their absence was very agreeable," reported the Board, although they had to send more provisions to the Creek encampment several days later, "which it was prudent to let them have." The incident was over, but not before it exposed the balance of power between European and Indian on the southern frontier. Despite previous victories by South Carolina against Tuscaroras, Yamasees, and Apalachees, southern planters feared war with the mighty Creeks.[3]

The Board's accounts of the events of August 1749 lay the blame fully at the feet of Mary Bosomworth and her family. Whether her ego or her drunkenness was the greatest culprit is hard to ascertain. Those reports, however, were most probably written by Habersham, the new colonial secretary and not-so-coincidentally, the major benefactor of the summer, as all the provisioning of the Lower Creeks brought profit straight to him, perhaps to counter the lost monies from the regiment. Several years later, affidavits from Bosomworth's family would claim Habersham had been behind the whole scene, and not just for short-term gain. "The Disturbance and Confusion . . . at Savannah was purposely Created by some leading Men there who had their own Sinister Ends in View in Order to make the danger of an Indian Warr a Pretext for an Application to the Government to grant Forces for Georgia as James Habersham Merchant in Savannah at that time Publickly declared."[4] Indeed, in a ten-page letter to the Trustees describing the August "crisis," the Board had emphasized how vulnerable the colony was. "All our Neighbouring Indians but especially the Creeks are too sensible that our red wall [meaning General Oglethorpe's regiment] is broke down."[5] Yet, as one witness pointed out, the Lower Creeks brought their families to Savannah; they never came on a war footing, and no militia was needed. Mary Bosomworth finally won a deed for St. Catherines Island.[6]

Habersham did not succeed in bringing back a military occupation, although he continued to fill the occasional government contract, for provisioning visiting military boats or materials for public buildings. And soon enough he realized he could fare very well, anyhow. With the acceptance of slavery moving ahead of the official Royal decree of 1751, planters like Jonathan and Hugh Bryan flooded into Georgia with their slaves, and Harris and Habersham Inc. stepped up to meet their needs. After securing large tracts of land for himself and his sons, Habersham, with the help of his planter cronies, remade Georgia in the mirror image of South Carolina.[7]

■ Specific types of South Carolinians were prepared to move onto the frontier and especially into the area south of Savannah on the Great and Little Ogeechee Rivers. The disruption of the war had upset Atlantic trade in the mid-1740s, and rice prices took a nasty tumble. Those planters not in the top rank of Charles Town society suffered most, and some sought a fresh start in the region to the south. Whether they hoped to repay their debts or just escape the creditors, they asked Habersham's Board—for it was neither the Trustees' Board any longer nor the King's Board quite yet—for land. The more they seemed like the right sort, "known to be of sufficient Substance" as the Board liked to declare, the more land they received. The greatest rewards went to those who came early and helped with the transition to slavery and especially to those who had a personal relationship with Habersham, like the Bryan brothers. By May 1752, the Board was granting 500 acres each to the minor sons of Jonathan Bryan and Habersham, and specifying good quality tracts. Officers who had managed to make army life profitable, including one who had "acquired a pretty Fortune during his being in the Military Service," also received 500-acre tracts. Meanwhile ex-servants and demobilized soldiers outside of officer ranks tended to be allowed fifty-acre lots.[8] Alan Gallay's examination of the lands handed out shows that "those who possessed influence on the council were most likely to receive the best land . . . a small group of land barons monopolized Georgia's premier rice lands, while the rest of the population became dispersed throughout the colony."[9] By the Revolution, the richest 5 percent owned almost all of the most fertile lands in the premium locations. In 1752, some 3,000 white settlers constituted most of Georgia's population. By 1755, roughly 1,000 new whites and almost 2,000 enslaved people had joined them.[10]

Experienced in the Atlantic commercial world, Habersham understood better than anyone the advantage of moving as quickly as possible in the early 1750s. Without a Royal governor in place, no customs were collected in the port of Savannah, and so there was a "great advantage in having Negro's Imported free of Duty." Only those with good credit and connections could seize that short-lived opportunity, of course, before Governor John Reynolds arrived in 1754, and enforcement of the Navigation Acts began. By then, Habersham and Bryan had figured out what best served their purposes and presented Reynolds with a plan for the political economy of Georgia.

So long as Reynolds cooperated, that relationship went smoothly, and together they carved out huge swathes of lands for themselves. A table of lucrative fees for the governor and Secretary Habersham guaranteed a steady flow of ready cash into their pockets. The first hint of political dissent, by "Men of little or no Property," led to the prohibition of "tumultuous Assemblies and nightly Meetings" and a call upon Charles Town's planters to dispatch a "Sloop of War." The troublemakers were actually elected representatives of the people, calling for a town hall–type meeting in Savannah; as one observer noted, "There was not a broken Head or a bloody Nose" to report, but the days of free speech and assembly had come and gone. The Council soon appointed a public executioner as another deterrent to any notion of popular politics.[11]

However, Reynolds gradually revealed ideas of his own. The Georgia planters on his Council successfully petitioned London for his repeal—by now they had learned how to campaign on both sides of the Atlantic—and their victory showed their preeminence. It was "the single most important political event" of the Royal era, ensuring that Habersham and Bryan would accumulate as much as the richest men in the colonies.[12]

What then, for the victims? The slaves brought across the Atlantic in those terror ships, forced to work in the rice and, after the Revolution, cotton fields of Georgia, fearing the whip much less than the ever-present threat of the destruction of their family, survived the abuse and used the paternalistic condescension to establish churches where they were safe to express themselves. But their stories haunt American history and rip holes in the tapestries memorializing American liberty. When the sons of Habersham and Bryan and so many other southern planters joined the Patriot cause, they did so to protect their economic interests, especially slaveholding.

And the Trustees' charity cases and the poor whites from other colonies: what became of them in the new Georgia? By the end of the Trustee era, many had been convinced by the Malcontents and their relentless propaganda that slavery would benefit them too. Somehow the introduction of enslaved workers would bring a Charles Town level of prosperity that would seep down from those with capital to everyone else. They failed to understand that war had hampered development, not the existence of a free labor force; perhaps unaware of history and how the first generation of almost every colony had struggled in a frontier wilderness to get their economy moving without infrastructure such as roads and wharves, they bought the argument that racialized slavery would lift their boat. Perhaps some aspired to be great planters themselves. Like poor whites in the

Caribbean, they would be sorely disappointed, because the merchants would never extend the necessary credit. In the eighteenth century, in order to look like an English lord, wealth must be confined to a very few. "You will easily distinguish, that the People I refer to are really what you and I understand by Crackers," Habersham wrote another gentleman, about the poor whites on the frontier. Exclusivity is the very definition of status. Habersham, Bryan, and their ilk contrasted their lifestyles with the poor white "trash" as much as with their slaves and slept smugly and snugly in their sumptuous beds.[13]

Here we bought us two Servants, (viz.) an English Woman-Servant just come on Shore from a Ship of Leverpool, and a Negro Man-Servant; things absolutely necessary for all People that pretended to Settle in that Country.
—Defoe, *Moll Flanders*

In the spring of 1751, Bolzius sat down to answer a long questionnaire from one of the German benefactors of the Salzburger community, who showed some interest in joining the American planter class. Resigned by now to the new order, the pastor advised that "there is a great difference between those colonists who come here quite poor and those who bring some wealth," because the chances for the former set were now diminished. However, those who had capital could anticipate that "the life of the noblemen on the land in Germany to be similar in some respects to the life of our plantation owners," maintaining a self-sufficient estate. Not exactly the same, of course; Bolzius warned against transporting butlers, valets, and the like.[14] In the particular circumstances of the colonial South, white workers were both pushed and pulled away from household service. Pushed by racist values to associate domestic service with those lower on a human scale and pulled by the "great freedom of the country," whereby they could run to another colony or city and demand higher wages.[15]

For white men, it might have seemed 1750s Georgia could boast of an environment, culture, and economy that portended opportunity, if not the nobility's luxurious lifestyle. Even after twenty years of European settlement, the forests marveled the eyes. Peaches, plums, pears, and fig trees flourished with little care. Firs, oaks, gum trees, poplars, laurels, chestnuts, and cypresses abounded, all ready for timbering and marketing around the globe. Fish and fowl flourished in the rivers and woods. Once farmers grasped the differences in soils and seasons and amended practices accordingly, fruit, vegetables, and herbs of enormous variety grew in plenty.

Maize's yield per acre still astounded, although settlers battled worms and rot as they tried to store such crops; the stifling humidity attracted microscopic bugs as well as the mosquitoes and chiggers that feasted on humans and livestock. An aspiring poet would write of Georgia a few decades later,

> Their is one thing more attends this place
> Which we do call an Evil
> When we make Corn Wheat & Rice
> Its Eaten by the Weavel.[16]

Most lived in the simplest of homes, no more than twenty-four by sixteen feet, one story high and one room deep or in a dogtrot pattern with an open passage separating two pens. The architecture of Tidewater plantation houses so often associated with the eighteenth century was rarely seen in the colony. Built on wood foundations or with merely dirt floors, the houses needed but did not necessarily receive protection from termites and dampness, so they did not survive long. (Even crucial public buildings, such as the Tybee lighthouse and the first Savannah jail, eroded faster than the colony could keep up.) Bolzius recommended limestone as a building material to caulk the yellow pine boards, although some used burned oyster shells. Carpenters set imported window glass cut into nine-by-eleven-inch panes into the homes of only the more prosperous because glass was expensive. Homemade candles, half beeswax, half cattle fat, lit the dark rooms. The fire risk had to be carefully monitored. By the 1770s, the governors and prosperous planters erected homes to reflect their status.[17]

Garnering enough food still challenged the poorest. But now that the first generation had learnt from the hardships of the early years, if one could claim land, subsistence would not be as capricious as in Europe. Those slightly better off grew all manner of calorie-dense foods and developed recipes from the native crops, some tastier than others. Cornbread with butter replaced European wheat flour bread, and breakfasts often consisted solely of hominy. "Peanuts and potatoes are not the same thing," Bolzius explained to his friends back in Germany, and as he noted, new arrivals to the Americas enjoyed the flavors of both the nuts and sweet potatoes, the latter fried. Both were extremely nutritious, although he did warn of the side effect of "much wind." Georgians augmented the carbohydrate-heavy diet with sugar-laden beverages. Rather than beer, they chose "to make a brew out of water, sugar cane brandy (called rum), and sugar." Some added Florida orange juice, in a colonial version of the

"Cuban screw." Even the Pietists thought drinking straight water "without beer, brandy, or wine is not good for the hard workers."[18]

Not a life entirely of cocktails and nuts, eighteenth-century Georgians would continue to deal with the debacle of health care. When a boat suspected of carrying smallpox victims pulled into Tybee's harbor, everyone on board was quarantined. Any object they needed to transmit must be proffered on "a long cleft Stick . . . dipped in Vinegar, and afterwards smoaked before the Person receiving the same do touch it." Stephens reported "an American Distemper called the Dry Gripes," an intestinal failure. Scientist Benjamin Franklin's studies indicated this illness was due to lead poisoning from the heavy use of lead in pots, pans, and the stills that produced rum. Malaria would confound the doctors for decades to come, and yellow fever epidemics, much more dangerous but confined to urban spaces, raged sporadically in Savannah until after the Civil War. The best-educated men in Georgia had decided by the 1750s that changeable weather, in combination with the foolishness of drinking water undiluted with alcohol during or after a hot, hard day's work, induced "diarrheas and dysentries."[19]

Seasoning in colonial Georgia meant that with every year spent in the colony, one seemed to grow less subject to the fevers and fluxes that beset new migrants. Although yellow fever sporadically raged through Charleston and the other larger port cities of the British colonies, Trustee-era Savannah mercifully escaped that particular malady, which made its victims "turn yellow, hemorrhage very violently, and die, and then they turn black." We understand now that many early Georgians did suffer from malaria, but humans do develop a type of immunity to it with repeated exposure. Gradually, the survivors inured to the worst symptoms; "now it does not seem as bad as during the first years," Bolzius noted in 1748. Lest anyone enjoy glorious good health, however, other afflictions stepped up to torture the settlers. "Red dysentery" killed two of Habersham's daughters one week in July. Dysentery, often called "bloody flux" in the colonial period, resulted from the poor sanitation of the era, and the ugly effects were constant diarrhea, filled with pus and blood.[20] And in the late 1740s, Ebenezer children started eating dirt.

They did not stop at raw earth; suddenly, "linen, coal, leaves, paper . . . ashes, clay" looked delicious, too, and Rev. Bolzius despaired. Lacking any knowledge of modern medicine, of course, the community could not grasp that an iron deficiency (whether attributable to hookworm infection or an overreliance on corn) might bring on what doctors today label geophagy, a subset of pica, the eating of traditionally inedible substances. As more children died, adults confessed that they, too, found themselves drawn to consuming raw rice, beans, and corn. All the pastor could do was lecture on the sin of suicide. He realized the behaviors were not entirely voluntary, but remained mystified that while surrounded by an "over-abundance of peaches," someone might choose sand. The tragic loss of small children broke Ebenezer's heart and their pastor's only comfort at such funerals was that distress and adversity sent by God should bring "contrition" and "humility."[21] Later the children of Ebenezer gradually lost their taste for eating clay, but the practice would continue among the landless.[22]

While Bolzius struggled to help the children desire proper foods, the definition of suitable consumption lay within the parameters set by the deadly sin of gluttony. One resident abandoned Georgia for South Carolina, boasting "there he could eat meat three times a day," the pastor recorded. "He is like those who yearned for the fleshpots of Egypt while they were being tested in the desert." The physical body presented so many opportunities to sin. An ill woman in her delirium recalled "many serious transgressions" at dances back in Germany. Her feverishness perhaps emboldened her to challenge Bolzius; "if everybody who danced and enjoyed a good time were to be damned, only a few would find salvation," she cheekily pointed out. The pastor appreciated an exclusionary heaven, however.[23]

Travel throughout Georgia had become faster and easier as the price for horses fell sharply; "practically no Indian, his wife, and children walk on foot any longer." As horses became the common man's transport, the big planter would soon distinguish himself by his use of thoroughbreds and carriages. Unlike South Carolina, where road construction was much further advanced, in Georgia in 1751, the chief mode of transport remained boats and distances were indicated by water, rather than by the rare roads. Households might have a canoe for quick trips, but regular ferry services— flat-bottomed boats manned by several rowers—brought people back and forth across the Savannah or down from Charles Town. The riders who carried the vaguely regular mail between South Carolina and Georgia could move their horses on such ferries.[24]

Industry remained limited by the Navigation Acts, for as Bolzius simply explained, "goods which are manufactured in England must not be made in America for sale." Georgians had to import most metal tools, glass, and most of their cloth and that only from England, although the Salzburger settlers would have preferred the traditional tools found in Germany. The absence of British officials postponed the collection of customs in the early 1750s, but they would soon enforce the existing regulations and try to do so with the new duties passed in the 1760s, leading to the formation of the Sons of Liberty. The smuggling so widespread in other places never got much chance to develop in the port of Savannah, although illegally traded goods might eventually end up in the hands of southern colonists. Everyone was quite aware that merchants around the Caribbean ignored the empire's rules "without bad conscience," especially the 1733 Molasses Act, because most of the goods winding their way through several hands into the homes of Georgia were of the rum variety. Exports would mostly be farm produce including lumber, sent to the sugar islands, and skins from the Indian trade, mostly for European markets. Ships arrived into Charles Town harbor for the rice harvest at Christmas, spending January in the South, before delivering their cargoes to the southern coast of England in March. Small-scale silk manufacture provided some opportunities for poor women, especially those of Ebenezer who continued to produce until the Revolution. Cattle needed fencing to bring a profit. Otherwise the wolves posed too much of a threat.[25]

Currency shortages still stultified internal trade in the colony, and a store credit economy was the general rule. The Trustees' sola bills circulated, and Habersham even printed his own money, small bills to facilitate business, further evidence of his power in the local economy. Carolina's paper money was accepted, but merchants often clung to these and made the farmers bringing their produce take goods from their stores in exchange. Spanish and Portuguese gold and silver coins and occasionally Dutch and French gold all served as legitimate currencies if one could attain them. The difficulties of finding a medium of exchange did not prevent the Indian traders in Augusta from continuing their lively business; one visitor described Augusta in 1753 as "an attractive and gay town . . . the merriest and best town in all of Georgia." In fact, for the first few years after the ban on slavery was lifted, Augusta's deerskins remained the most lucrative business. But most of the shipping went through Charles Town until the 1760s. Much of it had been exchanged for rum.[26]

As the laws stood in 1751, craftsmen and their high wages should be protected from being pushed to the margins by slavery. One of the deals made to secure poor whites' yielding of slavery was the promise that all skilled work would be restricted to white men. Salzburgers understood how empty and unenforceable such a promise was; "as happened in Carolina, the neighboring province, poorer people will not be able to get by," wrote one back to Germany. Some specialists might develop successful businesses in Savannah over the next century (e.g., butchers and bakers, or perhaps taverners), but most big planters happily had their slaves learn the important skills needed around the estate, such as carpentry and smithing. Working-class white men instead found work as overseers, doing the nasty work of brutalizing the only people poorer than themselves, while the big planters kept their consciences clean and appeared to be benevolent patriarchs, alleviating the worst cruelties of the men they had hired to be cruel.[27]

At the bottom end of the scale, Bolzius noted, newly enslaved Africans "frequently take their own lives out of desperation." To enquiries about security, he counseled of the need for enough white overseers, for less-depressed slaves might kill or head out for St. Augustine. Deterrents included horrific punishments for any slave considered an agitator who might endure the fate of being "slowly roasted at the fire." Since Stono, "one goes to church with swords, guns and pistols." Single young men must especially be controlled, whereas enslaved people with spouses or children "love their families dearly and none runs away from the other," and thus posed less risk. Bolzius explained that the new rules for slavery in Georgia forbade the breakup of families, but explained the Carolina definition of slave family soon to become the norm in Savannah. Children under the age of eight usually were sold along with their mothers, fetching £7 in addition to their mother's price. It was perfectly acceptable to sell anyone over eight years old, and by fifteen, bondspeople were classified as adult. The price of these children and adolescents depended on their health, and Bolzius guessed that those born in the Americas would bring a higher price than those who had just endured the Middle Passage, although Savannah did not attract slaving ships straight from Africa until the mid-1760s. The pastor could not address anything as taboo as pedophilia and how slavery automatically legalized such barbarities for anyone who could afford to simply purchase their victims, but he did mention that the slave women in Charles Town "who are mistresses, are very well dressed" compared to those who worked the fields. These women were often status symbols for their masters, in a society so patriarchal that married men had no need to hide them.[28]

Bolzius's longest response came to the question, "What is the daily work of the Negroes on a plantation throughout the year?" Clearing land of trees and fence building preceded cultivation even on the small-scale farm. Only describing what he knew of South Carolina, Bolzius did not fully comprehend the horrors of the physical labor of the tidal swamp method of growing rice, which required the construction of massive embankments made of marsh mud and the digging of drainage ditches. This work killed up to 5 percent of the enslaved each year, ensuring the Atlantic slave trade would continue. Once the slaves had transformed the environment, the planter imposed a regular annual routine. Potatoes first, then slaves should plant half an acre of corn per day. Rice followed in the heat of the summer and once sown, the laborers turned to weeding and planting beans amidst the corn. While the children tended the potatoes, adults maintained the acres of corn, rice, and beans, helped with housework, worked on the public roads, and might also be growing pumpkins and beets. At harvesttime, armed with sickles, they cut the crop before the brutal hand processing began. Without mills, slaves threshed with flails and then ground thousands of pounds of rice with wooden mortars and pestles. This by the undernourished and barely clothed, who returned exhausted to the cabins they had built. The intensity of such labor caused planters to worry about how much it weakened their ill-fed slaves, and gradually slaves on the low-country task system negotiated a set amount of labor that became almost universal. Over the Christmas season, slaves must plant peas, beans, and cabbage and prune any foliage necessary. In the few first few months of the year, they repaired fences or cleared new acreage for cultivation. Slaves perhaps looked forward to the less demanding seasons and to Sundays, when they had permission to fish, to plant rice, peanuts, and melons, and to raise poultry to supplement the meager food supply of potatoes; the rice too spoiled to sell; and the corn, without salt or fat, issued by the master. Occasionally they might also hire themselves out as boatmen, and enslaved women ran market stalls in Charles Town.[29]

Bolzius was contemptuous of the propaganda spun to justify the abuse of slave labor. "I have often been told that the Negroes cannot be taught anything, that they are stupid . . . [it is] an invention. . . . They are smart enough, and can learn crafts and arts, also writing and arithmetic." The many entrepreneurial slaves who bought and sold produce and livestock throughout the colonial and antebellum periods, despite a stream of legislation designed to control such behaviors, supported Bolzius's depiction.[30]

What of the theory of "no alternative"? In a colonial domino theory, some historians asserted that, despite all the horror that slavery brought, a slave society in Georgia was inevitable.[31] An all-white colony never attracted enough settlers to be viable when the affluence of nearby Charles Town contrasted so sharply. The boom in population post-1750 apparently proves that the Trustees' goal, however laudable, was utopian. It bears examination. Did Savannah's struggles result from the labor situation? Or was this a case of geographical determination, where the heat dictated both the crops and the harvesters?

The first assumption is, of course, that the whole colony struggled. Certainly, Savannah was not booming; no great planters financed the beautiful homes and gardens that attract tourists today until slavery became legal. But elegant architecture and enchanting flowers often mask the ugliest of realities. What Raymond Williams has taught us from his examination of English manor houses applies to southern planters' homes, too.

> The social order within which this agriculture was practiced was as hard and as brutal as anything. . . . The uncountable thousands who grew crops and reared beasts only to be looted and burned and led away with tied wrists. . . . Think it through as labour and see how long and systematic the exploitation and seizure must have been. . . . What these "great" houses do is to break the scale, by an act of will corresponding to their real and systematic exploitation of others. For look at the sites, the facades, the defining avenues and walls, the great iron gates and the guardian lodges. These were chosen for more than the effect from the inside out. . . . They were chosen also, as you now see, for the other effect, from the outside looking in: a visible stamping of power, of displayed wealth and command: a social disproportion which was meant to impress and overawe. Much of the real profit of . . . agriculture went not into productive investment but into that explicit social declaration: . . . exposition, at every turn, of an established and commanding class power.[32]

In Georgia, we must add racial to that final sentence on class. Just as women's labor inside their homes is so often invisible, none of the statues erected in Savannah's exquisite squares honors the sweat and pain of those who actually built the houses or cut the trees and turned the soil in the gardens. And the monuments to the select few do not indicate prosperity for many. The voices of most of the original charter group have been silenced.

Gauging the economic success of colonial southerners depends on the populations one chooses to contrast. Comparing newly founded Savannah to Charles Town sixty years after its birth was a ruse to make regular people on both sides of the Atlantic look askance at the Georgian city, both at the time and ever since. Clearing the lands along the coast of South Carolina had taken Indian and African slaves decades. That sick Londoners had not caught up in fifteen years should be no surprise.

A better analogy is found in Purrysburg, South Carolina, a township settled on the other side of the Savannah River twenty-five miles from Savannah at precisely the same moment the Trustees launched their colony.

In many ways, the story of Purrysburg serves as an excellent alternative universe: another 1730s refuge for the poor of Europe, with the striking difference that slavery was legal. According to the Malcontents, that alone should have guaranteed economic success.

Arlin Migliazzo painstakingly researched the story of Purrysburg from its founding in 1732 through the Civil War. Swiss entrepreneur Jean Pierre Purry's ideas for a personal southern fiefdom did not match the Trustees' perfectly: he sought wealth and status for himself and dreamed of a life of aristocratic grandeur in South Carolina. But the practicalities of the settlement for those who moved were remarkably similar to those who went to Georgia. Poor people, promised their own land, emigrated from Europe to the steamy country and fought to produce a sufficiency on a terrain and in a climate entirely foreign, while powerful planters in Charles Town viewed them merely as a protective buffer from the Spanish. "From every vantage point it is apparent that the creation of Purrysburg Township served the interests of entrenched provincial elites at the expense of the colonists to be."[33]

The small farmers in South Carolina faced almost every problem of those in Georgia. Malaria, worsened by poor nutrition that led to beriberi, was rampant through the township, inflicting as awful a mortality rate as in Savannah in those first two decades. Medical "experts" prescribed vomiting or mercury, among other treatments. Many children of Purrysburg ended up at the orphanage in Ebenezer. The shock and horror of such a demographic disaster surely had the same demoralizing effect on the residents in South Carolina as it did further south. Legal slavery offered no consolation.[34]

Slavery, however, or at least according to the several bands of Malcontents, promised tremendous differences in economic outcomes on either side of the Savannah River. Purrysburg residents should have been quickly thriving, watching Africans haul in huge loads of rice and indigo for the Atlantic trade shipping in and out of Charles Town as they counted their money, while the wretched settlers in Georgia struggled to survive with only white labor. Yet all accounts indicate the very opposite state of affairs. After a few years of settlement, Purrysburg men made their way by boat to Savannah for work, needing to earn some of those high wages Tailfer and his cronies complained of. Thomas Causton, the beleaguered Trustee storekeeper in the mid-1730s, described them as "some of the poor people at Purrysburg who were in a very low condition," nearly four years after the founding of the township. The following year, Bolzius's Salzburgers began to employ Purrysburg carpenters and other craftsmen and laborers to help build mills. They enjoyed even higher wages as war with Spain pulled men into the military and made their skills more valuable.[35]

So why did they not purchase slaves and live in luxury like Charles Town grandees? At the very least, one might have expected that the rice profits bringing wealth to those great planters would have circulated, giving opportunities to the newcomers. The answer is found in the land accumulation of those same planters who had laid claim to all the best arable lands in the region, stymieing any possibility that poor white farmers might join their class.[36] Absentees all, but smart enough to understand real estate markets, South Carolina's planters and their expansionist philosophy never intended to benefit all white men. They had no more regard for the struggling Purrysburg settlers than for their slaves. The township, like the Trustees' colony, buffered the elite against Spanish incoming and slave outgoing.

Gradually, the absentee landowners purchased the lands in and around Purrysburg from the original settlers and their children and moved their slaves into the region. Only five families of those who had come with Purry managed to see some prosperity in the area. Unable to compete with those in command of capital and credit in Charles Town, most of the survivors made their way to Georgia seeking a fresh start.[37] A few would prosper there, but for the majority of whites in the Deep South, slavery, whether in South Carolina or Georgia, trapped them in a poverty alleviated only by the psychological balm of white supremacist belief. Social mobility was somewhat more possible in all colonies than in lineage-bound Europe; the availability of land and the absence of nobility ensured that. Yet a revolution was needed to bring equality of opportunity to colonial white men. Only when they needed poor white support for the Revolution did the big planters of South Carolina concede any measure of political power and then less than the elites of any other state. The Revolution in the South was firmly held under the auspices of the planters to ensure their continued control of all the political and legal institutions. Instead, their policy of divide and conquer nurtured a racism that emphasized the differences between those at the bottom. Purrysburg's story highlights the reality that enslaving others did not raise all white boats.

Timothy Lockley's work *Lines in the Sand* traces the interactions of non-slaveholding whites and African Americans in Georgia after the Trustee era. "Poor farmers and laborers often found themselves economically marginalized, forced by slavery into a subsistence existence," he explains, often forced to supplement their diet through hunting. Held in complete disdain by the planters, the "tattered appearance and hand-to-mouth existence of rural nonslaveholders" laid bare the reality of the Malcontents' false theories. The extremes of class stratification in Georgia until after the Civil War prove slavery's evils served a tiny percentage.[38] Although much of the North brought in some level of free and compulsory education after the Revolution to guarantee an electorate with powers of critical thinking, southern planters refused to introduce such a system. Instead education came from the pulpit. The evangelical churches, founded in Savannah on a theology of the lowly Christ and once a major source of the questioning of deference, contorted themselves into "the ideal forum for the dissemination of a message [that] . . . slavery and social hierarchy . . . were divinely ordained."[39]

The reputation of post-Trustee Georgia as a success also depends on the notion that the colony finally stood on its own feet once the legalization of slavery attracted large numbers of settlers. This too is myth; as a Royal colony, the British Parliament continued to subsidize Georgia's government because "the likelihood of the inhabitants' being able to support themselves tended to recede rather than improve." Annual subsidies in the Royal era of between £3,000 and £4,000 to pay the salaries of government officials equaled the last few grants awarded the Trustees, who had been forced to fight so hard to justify those expenditures in the face of Thomas Stephens's propaganda about wasted money. Indian gifts cost as much in the 1750s and 1760s as they had in the 1730s and 1740s. Quit-rents (a type of land tax), never paid in the Trustee period, remained uncollected during the Royal era. The colony was "British property" to a greater degree than any of the others on the American mainland, and the last of the thirteen to join the Continental Congress. The indebtedness of individuals to British merchants surpassed that of South Carolinians by 50 percent. Arguments that the introduction of slavery made Georgia viable lose water in the face of the arithmetic.[40]

We can also look to Pennsylvania as a comparative study. Founded in 1683 as a charter colony and with an underpinning of an egalitarian religion, the Quaker colony faced its share of trial and tribulation in its first few decades. Slavery was never outlawed, but neither was the colonial economy dependent upon bondspeople. Approximately 100,000 British and a further 70,000 Germans, most of them indentured servants, landed in Philadelphia in the mid-eighteenth century, after Georgia's founding.[41] Although they suffered, no one questions the viability of Pennsylvania as a political and economic entity. Could that model not have worked in Georgia? Why not? Had as many emigrants, free and temporarily unfree, been attracted to Georgia, could the Trustee vision have become reality?

John Smolenski's fascinating book, *Friends and Strangers*, examines the first generation of European settlers in Pennsylvania. He describes how a struggle ensued to define the political culture of the colony. Led by William Penn—like Oglethorpe, a powerful philanthropist on a mission to create an ideal society and willing to deal respectfully with Indian peoples—Pennsylvania attracted persecuted German Protestants of all stripes. In Quaker Philadelphia as in Savannah, the popular religious ethic emphasized social equality, even as those promoting it shied away from the political implications of that theology. Penn, like the Trustees and Whitefield, actually preferred "a deferential political society in which ordinary citizens easily recognized the superior leadership capabilities of the ruling class." Twenty years after the founding, Penn was in "utter despair" that his vision had not fully materialized, for the civic virtue he counted upon seemed to be terribly lacking in the denizens. Just like the Trustees, he sat in London, wondering why it had all gone wrong.[42] Yet Pennsylvania did grow, did gradually become a place for poor whites to throw off the shackles of Old World class rules, did take the lead in a revolution they thought would bring social equality, and did confront the hypocrisy of proclaiming Liberty while holding people in slavery.[43] None of these developments took place in Georgia. But that they did not was not inevitable.

Eighteenth-century concepts of climate, disease, and race all played a part in convincing the powerful in London that Georgia faced imminent collapse without the intervention of hard-working black people. Did the southern heat really melt pasty Europeans? Many complained that white servants could not function in the Georgia temperatures. But bosses in Philadelphia and on the farms around the region also complained about lazy servants and laborers demanding too much money, as they did in Savannah and everywhere else, throughout time and place. Even in cool New England, Martha Ballard whined endlessly about the servant girls' tendencies to avoid a hard day's work. One can ever hear some version of the refrain, "You just can't get the help these days."[44] Poor farmers of the Trustee period did find it extremely difficult to make the Georgia land work for them, but no basket of bread came easily in Pennsylvania either. Indentured servants supplemented the family labor.

Rice produced much greater profit margin, but could only grow in the southern climate and wet soils. Planters claimed white children could not produce rice; only African hands could dig the ditches and canals through the snake- and alligator-ridden swamps and, of course, cope with the inescapable malarial fevers. Salzburgers mocked this claim: "We are told by several people, after our arrival, that it proves quite impossible and dangerous for white people to plant and manufacture any rice, being a work only for Negroes, not for European People. But . . . we laugh at such a tale, seeing that several people of us have had in last Harvest, a greater crop of rice than they wanted for their own consumption." However, to wrest the huge profits, most believed that a labor force of less than thirty could not prove capable of the ditching and dam building a successful rice plantation required.[45]

The more important audience for the argument was the European peasantry considering a fresh start in the New World. The migrants from southwestern Germany and Switzerland were leaving societies "nearly destroyed" by the Thirty Years War. The process of state building that followed in the eighteenth century gave rulers even greater powers of taxation. As the population exploded, land-poor peasants contemplated leaving their homelands. The region attracted boosters from eastern Europe as well as those selling America as a destination, and indeed, only about 15 percent of migrants took the chance of the Atlantic crossing, half of those coming as indentured servants. They could have come to Georgia and moved off into the interior, where a variety of less labor-intensive crops could flourish. But the vast majority chose Pennsylvania instead, and that choice cannot be ascribed merely to climactic preferences.[46] All the letters and journals Bolzius wrote and the petitions his community signed could not balance the unrelenting drone of negativity emanating from South Carolina through the Atlantic networks. The Charles Town elite mounted a multifaceted campaign to expand their rice-and-slaves empire. They needed some poor whites, certainly, to help manage the vast numbers of desperate enslaved, so they happily accepted the runaway servants from Georgia, but they needed to discredit the idea that a society without slaves might function. The war with Spain in the southern colony meant disruption of labor and harvests so frequently that the campaign of the Malcontents appeared to have merit. "Georgia has been, in times past, a despised land . . . in comparison with Carolina," the pastor explained. Once slavery became legal, "the disdain has stopped and many Carolina and Virginia gentlemen transport themselves and their families to us."[47]

Slavery certainly made agriculture generally more profitable, despite the initial cost. Contemporaries estimated that the purchase of a slave, although perhaps five times more costly than an indenture, paid for itself quickly, because the outlay for food and clothing amounted to about 25 percent of the annual expenditure on a white servant. "The upkeep of the Negroes is cut very sparse . . . If they have benevolent masters, or prove themselves loyal, they may receive a little meat a few times a year," observed Bolzius. "Benevolent masters" referenced Bryan and Habersham, friends of the Ebenezer pastor by dint of their devout Christian worship, whose professed amelioration of slavery through a combination of less brutality and the promise of rewards in a Christian afterlife did not extend to granting even a minimum wage. So after providing the minimum of necessities, masters could budget for a profit of £10 per year from each "industrious Negro," and even more later in the century.[48] Yet only a few with access to capital or credit could ever hazard the initial investment of £30 to buy an adult slave. In Purrysburg, one would-be planter bought three men on credit. Two died, one by suicide, and the third became seriously disabled in his attempt to escape, leaving the farmer buried in debt.[49] On the other hand, farmers throughout Pennsylvania made profits, and yeomen across the South would comfortably feed their families from the colonial period to the twentieth century. The distinction between need and desire was often blurry in the minds and words of planters.

■ Georgia set off down the path laid by the South Carolinian elites. Migration increased, the infrastructure developed, import and export numbers reflected a growing commerce: all signs of a more vibrant economy and thus a "viable," perhaps even "successful," colony. Such statistics disguised a hard reality. While enslaved people eked out a life under constant threat of violence and broken families, most free peoples' lives held little security, let alone hope of prosperity. Fooled by a relentless and ruthless propaganda that claimed the mistreatment of others would bring enrichment, most Georgians acquiesced to the slave society. Few would find their boat lifted.

CONCLUSION

Some might say the discussion of potential outcomes from Trustee Georgia is moot; Georgia developed into a slave society and remained so until William Tecumseh Sherman crossed the state line in 1864 and his union troops marched through the colony. For another century after that, many American citizens in the state were prevented from pursuing happiness, politically and economically. This suppression is not a history the current generation, raised in more enlightened times, can look to with pride. But they can look to it for lessons on building a better future Georgia, where words like "liberty" and "equality" can be uttered with sincerity.

If we face the possibilities open to colonial settlers, we must examine why a particular choice was made and ascribe responsibility for that choice. Most white people of the charter group saw the advantages they held under the Trustee plan: free land, high wages, and the freedom to hunt on horseback like the king. The liminal space of the frontier allowed people oppressed in their homeland greater flexibility to control their own destiny. They proved capable of thinking critically about the Malcontents' arguments through the 1730s. But they could not hold out forever against the relentlessness of the planter class.

Lacking the organization, the eloquence, or the connections to corridors of power in Whitehall, the poor in Georgia depended on Trustees with whom they shared no class values. Those Trustees expected deference, however: a working class who would concede that elites are more virtuous and wise and whose decisions, no matter how inappropriate for a marshy wilderness, should not be questioned. Disillusioned with charity cases who dared pursue their own goals, those "Day Labourers" demanding the wages the labor market would bear, the Trustees lost faith. Poor peoples' voices fell silent. Finally persuaded by an unyielding powerful group that slaves in Georgia would improve their standard of living, they acquiesced.

Let us not judge the people at the bottom of today or of yesteryear. Those with few options, such as poor white settlers scrabbling hard to ensure their survival, must do what they can. If one feels one must betray a friend to earn food for one's child, who can stand in judgment? Wealth and power carry choices, however, and with choice comes responsibility. Those who had the option of a much more secure place, yet were prepared to accommodate their conscience to their ambition, must face greater scrutiny. Planters such as Habersham and those of South Carolina won the battle for status and closed the door to the social staircase behind them for two hundred years.

■ The cultural cost of slavery to white people—part of the creolization of Georgia culture from Anglo-Saxon to something distinctly American— has to be measured in a way that includes the twisting of Christianity from a religion for the meek and the peaceful into one that could incorporate churchgoers armed with implements of oppression. (The Bible remains a malleable text.) To Bolzius in 1745, this stance was unfathomable. But planters, and increasingly, white non-slaveholders, found a way to make their peace with it, to tell themselves that devout Christianity could be reconciled with buying and selling other peoples' children for money. They told themselves, their children, and any who came to visit that God sanctioned slavery, citing select Old Testament stories and carefully omitting the plagues sent to Egyptian slave owners. They patted themselves on the back as they explained that plantations were not slave labor camps, but just another type of family household, with a benevolent father figure at the head. If slaves had better opportunity to save their souls through the Christian Gospels than they might have found in Africa, well then, a greater good was served.

More immune than most of us to material temptation, Bolzius could say "the value of beautiful mirrors with beautiful frames is unknown to me" and mean every possible interpretation of that sentence. Yet even he and many others of the most pious, the most sincere devotion to the lowly Christ succumbed to the temptation of enslaving others to bring themselves greater wealth. Bolzius bought five slaves in the spring of 1753, and other Ebenezer residents followed suit.[1]

Perhaps the biggest lesson for modern students of the past is not so much to pass judgment on the people of the past, but to grasp the power of humans to self-delude, to salve their consciences in the midst of cruelty and evil. The stories we tell ourselves about others and about ourselves to justify exploitation at home or abroad that sponsors a higher living standard must be subjected to the same power of critical thinking that we use on the slave-trade merchants. How do we reconcile conscience and the

American capitalism that drives human endeavor, supposedly raising all boats and rewarding hard work? We often evaluate the past from the perspective of our present situation and feel that if our current economic status is comfortable, then everything happened for a good reason. Such a presentist approach leads us to gloss over lessons we might learn from a detailed examination of the machinations of power, lessons we might apply to our own world.

If the "Day Labourers" had understood more sharply how philanthropists can lose interest and allow their good intentions to wander to the next cause, if they had education enough to articulate their arguments, if they had sent a spokesman to London as the Charles Town grandees did, they might have been capable of preserving a colony (and then state) where in fact they could have become "Masters," not of others, but of their own fates. Instead, their story has mostly been lost in the adoration of planter heroes and the agonies of race relations. Free Georgia, the era between 1733 and 1750, represents a moment of possibility for the South: the road not taken.

Notes

Abbreviations

CRG   Allen D. Candler et al., eds. *The Colonial Records of the State of Georgia*. Vols. 1–19, 21–26. (Atlanta: Franklin Printing and Publishing Company, 1904–1916).
Kenneth Coleman et al., eds. *The Colonial Records of the State of Georgia*. Vols. 20, 27–32. (Athens: University of Georgia Press, 1976–1989).

Egmont   Robert McPherson, ed., *The Journal of the Earl of Egmont: Abstracts of the Trustees' Proceedings for Establishing the Colony of Georgia, 1732–38*. (Athens: University of Georgia Press, 1962).

GHQ   *Georgia Historical Quarterly*

Urlsperger George F. Jones and Renate Wilson, eds., *Detailed Reports on the Salzburger Emigrants Who Settled in America, Edited by Samuel Urlsperger*. Vols. 6–12, 1739–48 (Athens: University of Georgia Press, 1981).

WMQ   *William and Mary Quarterly*

WSJ   Journals of William Stephens, 1737–45. 4 vols.: Vols. 1 and 2, William Stephens, *A Journal of the Proceedings in Georgia* (Readex Microprint); Vols. 3 and 4, E. Merton Coulter, ed., *The Journal of William Stephens, 1741–43* and *The Journal of William Stephens, 1743–45* (Athens: University of Georgia Press, 1958–59).

Introduction

1. Paula R. Backscheider, "Crime Wave and *Moll Flanders*," in Defoe, *Moll Flanders*, 460–71.

2. Natalie Zacek, "Class Struggle in a West Indian Plantation Society," in *Class Matters*, ed. Middleton and Smith, 63; Thompson, *Customs in Common*.

3. Konstantin Dierks, "Middle-Class Formation in Eighteenth-Century North America," in *Class Matters*, ed. Middleton and Smith, 103–5.

4. Thompson, *Customs in Common*, 16–72, quotation, 72; Linebaugh, *London Hanged*.

5. Braund, *Deerskins and Duffels*.

6. I stand on the shoulders of many historians. The standard monographs addressing many aspects of life in a chronology of the Trustee-era include Reese, *Colonial Georgia*; Coleman, *Colonial Georgia;* Davis, *Fledgling Province*. Jackson and Spalding, *Forty Years of Diversity,* brought to light newer research. Many historians have since examined one aspect or another of the period, such as slavery in Wood, *Slavery*

in Colonial Georgia, and Indian perspectives in Sweet, *Negotiating for Georgia,* and Juricek, *Colonial Georgia and the Creeks.* I sought a more inclusive story than the older studies and scoured the records for insights into the attitudes of the poor settlers from England, Scotland, and Germany who composed the majority in the colony. For a fuller historiographical essay, see Sweet, "Thirteenth Colony in Perspective."

Chapter One

1. Defoe, *Moll Flanders,* 383.

2. Linebaugh, *London Hanged,* 13.

3. Thomas, *House of Care,* 140–42. Oglethorpe surely was familiar with *Moll;* the novel was into its third edition by 1724 and was also serialized. Defoe was the most famous writer of the era. Paula R. Backscheider, "Crime Wave and *Moll Flanders,*" in Defoe, *Moll Flanders,* 471.

4. Russell, *Oglethorpe and Colonial Georgia,* 3–8.

5. Brundage, *English Poor Laws,* 12.

6. Clive Holmes, "Drainers and Fenmen: The Problem of Popular Political Consciousness in the Seventeenth Century," in *Order and Disorder,* ed. Fletcher and Stegenson, 166–95; Thompson, *Whigs and Hunters,* 21–24.

7. Thompson, *Whigs and Hunters,* 63–64, 104.

8. Ibid., 49.

9. Ibid., 197, 158, 172–73.

10. Ibid., 186–89.

11. Ibid., 77.

12. Beattie, *Policing and Punishment,* 384–88.

13. McGowen, "Well-Ordered Prison," 80–83.

14. Benjamin Martyn, "Reasons for Establishing the Colony of Georgia, 1733," in *Most Delightful Country,* ed. Trevor Reese, 159–98; Taylor, *Georgia Plan,* 16–23. Taylor's report has never been published as a monograph. However, his thorough research supported his identification of a few planters and their professional lobbyist Thomas Stephens as responsible for Georgia's switch to a slave society. I agree with Taylor's conclusions, but seek to explore further the goals and dreams of poor white colonists on the ground.

15. Meroney, "London Entrepot Merchants," 230–44.

16. Taylor, *Georgia Plan,* 17–18, 37, 304.

17. Ibid., 154–55; Reynes, *Couvent de femmes.*

18. Taylor, *Georgia Plan,* 14.

19. Benjamin Martyn, "An Account Shewing the Progress of the Colony of Georgia in America from its First Establishment," in *Clamorous Malcontents,* ed. Trevor Reese, 186–89.

20. Taylor, *Georgia Plan,* 10–11.

21. *CRG* 2:47.

22. Taylor, *Georgia Plan,* 25.

23. The later antislavery movement would also argue that slavery eroded the morals of slaveholders. Wood, *Slavery in Colonial Georgia,* 3–7.

24. James Oglethorpe, "New and Accurate Account of the Provinces of South Carolina and Georgia, 1732," in *Most Delightful Country*, ed. Trevor Reese, 144–45.

25. Bannon, *Spanish Borderlands Frontier*, 107.

26. Memorial of Jean Pierre Purry, July 18, 1724, in *Most Delightful Country*, ed. Trevor Reese, 62. A long tradition of extolling the natural wonders of the American colonies dated back a century. Such boosterism had left potential investors skeptical.

27. Stewart, *What Nature Suffers to Groe*, 64–68, 90.

28. Ibid., 73; Silver, *New Face on the Countryside*, 28–31.

29. *CRG* 20:262.

30. Loewald et al., "Questionnaire," 235.

31. Stewart, *What Nature Suffers to Groe*, 70; Silver, *New Face on the Countryside*, 14–16.

32. McNeill, *Mosquito Empires*, 7.

33. Loewald et al., "Questionnaire," 250.

34. Gallay, *Indian Slave Trade*, 3; Weir, *Colonial South Carolina*, 47–73.

35. Thomas, *Slave Trade*.

36. Wood, *Black Majority*; Rucker, *River Flows On*, 94–96; Eltis, Morgan, and Richardson, "Black, Brown, or White?," 164–71; quotation from Thomas, *Slave Trade*, 502.

37. Berlin, *Many Thousands Gone*; Chaplin, *Anxious Pursuit*; Morgan, *Slave Counterpoint*, 83–101.

38. Bolzius, "Reliable Answer," 243–44.

39. Wood, *This Remote Part of the World*.

40. Weir, *Colonial South Carolina*, 80–82; Peter H. Wood, "The Changing Population of the Colonial South: An Overview by Race and Region, 1685–1790," in *Powhatan's Mantle*, ed. Waselkov, Wood, and Hatley, 38.

41. Landers, *Black Society in Spanish Florida*, 25–27.

42. Migliazzo, *To Make This Land Our Own*, 44.

43. Gallay, *Indian Slave Trade*.

44. Sweet, *Negotiating*, 16–21.

45. Ibid., 19–31.

46. Bolzius, "Reliable Answer," 232.

47. Oglethorpe, "New and Accurate Account," 117–18.

48. Sweet, *Negotiating*, 25–28.

49. Bolzius, "Reliable Answer," 232.

Chapter Two

1. Ian A. Bell, "*Moll Flanders*, Crime and Comfort," in Defoe, *Moll Flanders*, 415.

2. Kussmaul, *Servants in Husbandry*; Kulikoff, *From British Peasants*, 17–24.

3. George Peckham, quoted in Galenson, *White Servitude*, 5.

4. Galenson, *White Servitude*, 7–9.

5. Mathias, *Transformation of England*, 137.

6. Smith, *Colonists in Bondage*, 245. The book was originally published in 1947. He goes on to give thanks for tough conditions for the servants: "Perhaps it was a

fortunate thing that pioneer conditions were as difficult as they were . . . for the weak, diseased and unenterprising were not preserved. . . . There was a speedy winnowing of the vast influx of riffraff which descended on the settlements; the residue, such as it was, became the American people," 306.

7. Kenneth Coleman, "The Founding of Georgia," in *Forty Years of Diversity*, ed. Jackson and Spaulding, 15.

8. Gordon, *Journal*, 24.

9. Ibid., 40–41.

10. *Egmont*, 33.

11. Coulter and Saye, *List*, 8–10; Gordon, *Journal*, 45–46.

12. *CRG* 20:29; *WSJ* 3:253.

13. Elaine F. Crane, " 'I Have Suffer'd Much Today': The Defining Force of Pain in Early America," in *Through a Glass Darkly*, ed. Hoffman, Sobel, and Teinte, 71.

14. *CRG* 20:28–29, 246.

15. *WSJ* 3:25, 253; *Urlsperger* 6:217, 9:93–94.

16. Gordon, *Journal*, 63.

17. Davis, *Fledgling Province*, 86; *Urlsperger* 9:166.

18. *WSJ* 3:253.

19. McNeill, *Mosquito Empires*, 52–62.

20. Carp, *Rebels Rising*, 63.

21. *CRG* 20:319. This Georgian master's claim was a great exaggeration of his financial loss.

22. Coleman, *Colonial Georgia*, 36–40; *CRG* 20:122.

23. Cashin, *Guardians of the Valley*, 33–34; Edward J. Cashin, "Gentlemen of Augusta," in *Colonial Augusta*, 30–32; Heard Robertson and Thomas H. Robertson, "Town and Fort of Augusta," in *Colonial Augusta*, ed. Edward J. Cashin, 62; Fleming, *Autobiography of a Colony*, 1.

24. *Egmont*, 36; Gordon, *Journal*, 46–47.

25. Gordon, *Journal*, 46–48; Coulter and Saye, *List*, 20; *CRG* 20:28.

26. Landsman, *Scotland and Its First American Colony*, 18–23; *Egmont*, 35–36.

27. *CRG* 20:24.

28. Sweet, "A Misguided Mistake," 1–29; *Egmont*, 18; *CRG* 20:30.

29. *CRG* 20:129.

30. Ibid., 29:33–34.

31. *Egmont*, 39, 44; *CRG* 20:41.

32. Defoe described the process by which transported felons were sold while still on board the docked ship. Because Moll brought some of her ill-gotten gains with her, she immediately purchased freedom for her spouse and herself, not the fate of most.

33. Ekirch, *Bound for America*, 13; Kussmaul, *Servants in Husbandry*, 102–12; Defoe, *Moll Flanders*, 151.

34. Rodney M. Baine, "Oglethorpe's Forty Irish Convicts," in *James Edward Oglethorpe*, ed. John Inscoe, 47–60.

35. *CRG* 20:141.

36. Ibid., 20:127.

37. Coulter and Saye, *List*, 67, 91, 96, 100, 101.

38. Ibid., 20, 79, 90.

39. *CRG* 29:20.

40. Ibid., 20:125–26, 164–65; Coulter and Saye, *List,* 95; Sweet, "The Murder of William Wise," 1–23. Sweet is sympathetic to the Irish servants and questions their guilt, but does not tie the baby in with the murder. Riley's baby was born forty-two weeks after the murder; it is usual that a woman's first baby is born over a week past the due date. There would have been little opportunity for anyone else to father the child.

41. Coulter and Saye, *List,* 95; *CRG* 20:182–83, 273.

42. *CRG* 20:199, 214, 239.

43. Coulter and Saye, *List,* 9; *CRG* 20:246, 344; *Egmont,* 18.

44. *CRG* 20:245–47, 283–84.

45. Ibid., 20:173–74, 185, 197; Juricek, *Colonial Georgia and the Creeks.*

46. *CRG* 20:175–76, 283.

47. Ibid., 20:237–46, 253–55.

48. Ibid., 20:258, 269–73, 283–87.

49. Ibid., 20:258–59, 271–72.

50. Ibid., 20:286.

51. Ibid., 20:275, 285–86, 291.

52. Coulter and Saye, *List,* 73–74; *CRG* 20:344; Lane, *General Oglethorpe's Georgia,* 409, 412.

53. Coulter and Saye, *List,* 62–63; *CRG* 20:216, 233 (italics added). Bathurst's son later ran away to South Carolina to avoid paying his father's debts and was killed in the Stono Rebellion.

54. *CRG* 29:31.

55. Ibid., 20:187–88.

56. Ibid., 20:212.

57. Ibid., 20:134–35.

58. Ibid., 20:18, 194–95; Davis, *Fledgling Province,* 68, 85.

59. *CRG* 20:133, 144, 293; Bolzius, "Reliable Answer," 251.

60. *CRG* 20:364–67.

61. *Egmont,* 96.

62. Ibid., 107, 114, 117.

Chapter Three

1. Defoe, *Moll Flanders,* 226.

2. Daniel Defoe, "Party-Tyranny," in Salley, *Narratives of Early Carolina,* 219–64.

3. Gallay, "Origins of Slaveholders' Paternalism," and Jackson, "Hugh Bryan" both look at Whitefield's work in the South, considering its impact upon slavery in South Carolina. I will consider the ramifications of evangelism for poor whites in Georgia.

4. Thompson, *Making of the English Working Class,* 28–54.

5. Wesley, *Journal,* 1:24–27.

6. Hattersley, *Life of John Wesley,* 51–100, quotation, 91; Hempton, *Methodism,* 13–14.

7. Wesley, *Journal*, 1:20–25.

8. *CRG* 20:419.

9. Wesley, *Journal*, 1:66.

10. Ibid., 52; Morgan, "Judaism in Eighteenth Century Georgia," 42.

11. Patrick Tailfer, "A True and Historical Narrative of the Colony of Georgia in America," in *Clamorous Malcontents*, ed. Trevor Reese, 66.

12. Stark, *For the Glory of God*, 17–34.

13. Curnock, *John Wesley's Journal*, 28.

14. *WSJ* 1:58.

15. Ibid., 15.

16. Coulter and Saye, *List*, 5, 7, 10, 61, 66, 95.

17. *WSJ* 1:12.

18. Ibid., 16; Lane, *General Oglethorpe's Georgia* 2:422.

19. *WSJ* 1:20.

20. Ibid., 45–48; Coulter and Saye, *List*, 9, 66.

21. Lane, *General Oglethorpe's Georgia*, 2:328–29.

22. *CRG* 29:261.

23. Jones, *Salzburger Saga*, 9–29; Melton, "Alpine Miner," 101, 109–15.

24. Ibid., 14–25; *Urlsperger* 6:49.

25. Jones, *Salzburger Saga*, 29–42.

26. Parker, *Scottish Highlanders*, 52–57; *CRG* 5:241.

27. Wesley, *Journal*, 1:29–40; Pennington, "John Wesley's Georgia Ministry," 239–41.

28. *WSJ* 1:57–58.

29. Ibid., 78; Wood, *Slavery in Colonial Georgia*, 25.

30. Dalliamore, *George Whitefield*, 57–114; Whitefield, *Letters*, 19–21.

31. The Great Awakening literature is vast, such as Gaustad's classic, *The Great Awakening in New England*. Butler's article, "Enthusiasm Described and Decried," produced its own revival of interest in the topic, including more recent works such as Stout, *Divine Dramatist*; Crawford, *Seasons of Grace*; Hall, *Contested Boundaries*; Noll, *Rise of Evangelism*; Gura, *Jonathan Edwards*; and Kidd, *Great Awakening*. These works pay little attention to Whitefield's time in Georgia beyond issues with building and supporting the orphanage. The argument over the role of the Awakening in the Revolution is not pertinent to this work, but I will argue that Wesley and Whitefield's mission had important sociopolitical connotations in 1730s and 1740s Georgia.

32. Whitefield, *Letters*, 93.

33. *WSJ* 1:204–33; Lane, *General Oglethorpe's Georgia*, 2:467, 475.

34. *WSJ* 1:234–52.

35. Ibid., 287–88.

36. Whitefield, *Journals*, 99; James 1:9–11 (Authorized King James Version); Linebaugh, *London Hanged*, 16–18.

37. Whitefield, *Journals*, 96, 250.

38. Stout, *Divine Dramatist*, 71, 83.

39. *WSJ* 1:308.

40. Ibid., 381, 387–88, 423.

41. *Egmont*, 352–57; *WSJ* 1:285, 305–6; *CRG* 5:68–73.

42. Whitefield, *Letters*, 45; *WSJ* 1:309, 356, 425; *CRG* 5:67.

43. *WSJ* 1:344; Tailfer, "True and Historical Narrative," 77–78; *CRG* 5:178; Jackson, "Darien Antislavery Petition," 618–31; Wood, *Slavery in Colonial Georgia*, 29–30.

44. Jackson, "Darien Anti-Slavery Petition."

45. Lane, *General Oglethorpe's Georgia*, 2:397–99; Melton, "Alpine Miner," 129–30.

46. Lane, *General Oglethorpe's Georgia*, 2:388–89.

47. *WSJ* 1:395–96, 414–15, 437–38, 446, 448.

48. *Urlsperger* 6:35.

49. *CRG* 30:38; *WSJ* 2:51; Tailfer, "True and Historical Narrative," 90–91; *CRG* 5:213.

50. *WSJ* 1:419.

51. Defoe, *Moll Flanders*, 61–62.

52. Marsh, *Georgia's Frontier Women*, 25–32, 91.

53. Mary Musgrove's unusual position of power has won her several biographies. See Hahn, *Life and Times of Mary Musgrove*; Todd, *Mary Musgrove;* Baine, "Myths of Mary Musgrove"; Gillespie, "The Sexual Politics of Race and Gender: Mary Musgrove and the Georgia Trustees" in *Devil's Lane*, ed. Clinton and Gillespie.

54. Bonner, "Silk Growing"; *CRG* 30:161, 260.

55. *CRG* 30:138, 281, 322, 346; Lane, *General Oglethorpe's Georgia*, 2:326; Marsh, *Georgia's Frontier Women*, 58–59.

56. Sweet, *William Stephens*, 162–68; *CRG* 24:69, 187, 30:236.

57. Coulter and Saye, *List*, 11, 24, 25, 40, 57, 65, 70, 88; *WSJ* 2:451; *CRG* 20:275; Marsh, *Georgia's Frontier Women*, 67–69. The "sale" of Willoughby was based on the English custom of wife sales in lieu of divorce, which were very difficult for the poor to attain. The "sale," a ceremony that always had the consent of the woman, signified to the local community that the couple were not cuckolding the previous husband and that he had consented to the new union. See Thompson, *Customs in Common*, 409–44.

58. *WSJ* 2:25–26; *CRG* 24:336–40, 346.

59. *WSJ* 2:26–27.

60. John J. TePaske, "The Fugitive Slave Intercolonial Rivalry and Spanish Slave Policy, 1687–1764," in *Eighteenth-Century Florida*, ed. Samuel Proctor, 2–7.

61. Landers, *Black Society in Spanish Florida*, 25–33; *WSJ* 1:357–58.

62. *WSJ* 1:399, 402–3, 412, 2:76–78.

Chapter Four

1. Defoe pointed out the less visible cost of Britain's overseas empire. Widows left destitute might turn to prostitution. Many of the younger criminals in London were the orphans of soldiers and sailors. Paula R. Backscheider, "The Crime Wave," in Defoe, *Moll Flanders*, 464.

2. Reese, "Georgia in Anglo-Spanish Diplomacy"; *CRG* 5:98–131.

3. Smith, *Stono*, 29.

4. Peter Hoffer argues for a less organized "rebellion," proposing that the Stono Rebellion was a contingent set of actions by some members of a disgruntled drainage crew forced to work on a Sunday. However it began, the actions following the break-in at the store demonstrate that a large group of slaves were determined to free themselves and others. Hoffer, *Cry Liberty*; Thornton, "African Dimensions of the Stono Rebellion."

5. Smith, *Stono*, 8, 12; *WSJ* 2:128–30.

6. *WSJ* 2:129.

7. *Urlsperger* 6:226.

8. *CRG* 5:160; Lane, *General Oglethorpe's Georgia*, 2:475.

9. *WSJ* 2:199; *CRG* 30:76, 236, 243; Lane, *General Oglethorpe's Georgia*, 2:351.

10. John J. TePaske, introduction in Kimber, *Relation or Journal*, xxiii–xxiv; Killpatrick, *Impartial Account*, 11–12.

11. Ivers, "Battle of Fort Mosa," 135–38.

12. *CRG* 5:170.

13. Ivers, "Battle of Fort Mosa," 140–44.

14. Parker, *Scottish Highlanders*, 79–83.

15. Killpatrick, *Impartial Account*, 24–27.

16. *CRG* 5:143–48.

17. Ibid., 235–37; 259–61; 266–67; 274; 298–308; Wood, *Slavery in Colonial Georgia*, 32–35.

18. Stout, *Divine Dramatist*, 66–98; Dalliamore, *George Whitefield*, 432–42; Lambert, *Pedlar in Divinity*, 104–16; Hoffer, *When Benjamin Franklin Met the Reverend Whitefield*; Whitefield, *Letters*, 62–63.

19. The responsibility for orphans unclaimed by kin fell to the parish, who often assigned them to be servants at a very young age. This prospect terrified Moll. Most parishes in the colonies had no orphanages; small children were bound out as apprentices. "The majority of orphans did not get guardians . . . they got masters." Brewer, *By Birth or Consent*, 230–37.

20. Whitefield, *Letters*, 54, 76, 109.

21. Cashin, *Beloved Bethesda*; Whitefield, *Letters*, 105.

22. *WSJ* 2:248.

23. Whitefield, *Letters*, 152.

24. Lambert, *Habersham*, 37–50; Cashin, *Bethesda*, 19–21; *WSJ* 2:456.

25. Whitefield, *Letters*, 135, 138.

26. Whitefield, *Journals*, 248–51.

27. Olwell, *Masters, Slaves, and Subjects*, 50.

28. Parent, *Foul Means*, 236–64.

29. Whitefield, *Journals*, 259–60.

30. Jackson, "Hugh Bryan and the Evangelical Movement," 598–601.

31. Whitefield's letter is reproduced in Gallay, *Voices of the Old South*, 148–51. Rhys Isaac's work narrates their reactions in the 1760s when Baptists with similar values made headway in Virginia. Isaac, "Evangelical Revolt," 346–68.

32. James 5:1–5 (Authorized King James Version).

33. Stein, "George Whitefield on Slavery," 243–56.

34. *CRG* 5:347–48, 372; Coulter and Saye, *List*, 6, 40, 61, 76, 92; Wood, *Slavery in Colonial Georgia*, 220n21.

35. *CRG* 5:463; Cashin, *Guardians*, 42; Cashin, "Gentlemen of Augusta," in *Colonial Augusta*, 33–36; Helen Callahan, "Colonial Life in Augusta," in *Colonial Augusta*, ed. Edward J. Cashin, 97–100.

36. Their agent in London, however, failed to publish this report there, perhaps prevented from doing so by Governor Glen, who was building a relationship with the Georgia Trustees. Another South Carolinian who had read the original report summarized it and published it in 1742. Aileen Moore Topping, introduction in Killpatrick, *Impartial Account*, xiv–xxviii, 65.

37. *CRG* 5:380, 386, 394, 423.

38. Tailfer, "True and Historical Narrative," 28; *CRG* 5:398–99.

39. Egmont Papers, 14210, 166 (418).

40. Taylor, *Georgia Plan*, 158–68.

41. Tailfer, "True and Historical Narrative," quotations 24, 55, 57, 66–67, 120.

42. *CRG* 5:422–28, 432, 435–36.

43. Marsh, *Georgia's Frontier Women*, 23; *CRG* 5:451, 459, 465.

44. Benjamin Martyn, "An Impartial Enquiry into the State and Utility of the Province of Georgia," in *Clamorous Malcontents*, ed. Trevor Reese, 123–61; *CRG* 5:439–41.

45. *CRG* 5:463, 465, 475, 480, 489, 496, 592.

46. Ibid. 5:539–42, 570–71, 591, 605; Coulter and Saye, *List*, 32–35.

47. Whitefield, *Letters*, 197–200.

48. *WSJ* 2:270.

49. Ibid., 269–70.

50. Trustees to Bailiffs and Recorder of the Town of Savannah, Egmont Papers 14210, 545; Stout, *Divine Dramatist*, 109–10; Dalliamore, *George Whitefield*, 455–62; *CRG* 5:333, 359–60, 673; Cashin, *Bethesda*, 36, 41–42.

51. *CRG* 5:503; Jackson, "Hugh Bryan and the Evangelical Movement," 606–10.

52. Jackson, "Hugh Bryan and the Evangelical Movement," 610; Gallay, "Origins of Slaveholders' Paternalism," 388.

53. Taylor, *Georgia Plan*, 172–81, 204–22.

54. *CRG* 23:456–57; Wood, *Slavery in Colonial Georgia*, 29–30.

55. *CRG* 5:616–21, 632, 635–37.

56. Parker, *Scottish Highlanders*, 86–87.

57. Life in the lower military ranks was often seen as a last resort. But military contracts brought big financial rewards for commanders and contractors. Thompson, *Customs in Common*, 26.

58. Sturgill and Turner, "Importance of Being at War," 129–35.

59. Parker, *Scottish Highlanders*, 87–91; Ivers, *British Drums*, 151–66.

60. Harvey H. Jackson, "Behind the Lines: Oglethorpe, Savannah, and the War of Jenkins' Ear," in *James Edward Oglethorpe*, ed. John Inscoe, 91.

61. *CRG* 5:641–45, 648–50, 679; Wood, *Slavery in Colonial Georgia*, 9.

Chapter Five

1. *CRG* 5:654–55, 687, 24:95–97, 163.
2. Ivers, *British Drums*, 196–200; *CRG* 5:687, 24:27, 95; *WSJ* 4:164.
3. *CRG* 5:674, 691, 6:55–58, 83, 86–87, 120, 24:42, 207; *WSJ* 4:4, 24, 38, 59–60.
4. *CRG* 24:187, 207; *WSJ* 4:51.
5. Ivers, *British Drums*, 175–82; Sweet, *Negotiating for Georgia*, 152–53.
6. *CRG* 5:693, 696, 705–8, 30:278–84, 317; *WSJ* 4:5; Taylor, *Georgia Plan*, 226; Ettinger, *Oglethorpe*, 71–75.
7. *WSJ* 4:14, 252; Lambert, *Habersham*, 14–23, 59–60; Cashin, *Bethesda*, 5.
8. Lambert, *Habersham*, 56–58, 62, 92; Cashin, *Bethesda*, 38; *CRG* 6:105; *CRG* 24:225, 334, 242–43, 291–92.
9. *CRG* 24:246–67, 285.
10. Ibid., 24:253–54.
11. Ibid., 24:254–55, 283–85; *WSJ* 4:3.
12. *CRG* 6:144, 207–8, 241–42, 25:20–23, 33.
13. Ibid., 24:382–84; *WSJ* 4:230.
14. Ivers, *British Drums*, 196–200; Lane, *General Oglethorpe's Georgia*, 2:343.
15. Ivers, *British Drums*, 196–200; *CRG* 30:221.
16. *CRG* 24:224–25, 425–26, 30:290–91.
17. Ibid., 24:49–50, 61–64, 115–16, 268.
18. Ibid., 24:313, 316, 334, 353, 355.
19. Ibid., 24:333–34, 342, 367–68.
20. Ibid., 24:342, 349–51, 393, 431; *WSJ* 4:24.
21. *CRG* 24:342, 378; *WSJ* 4:118.
22. *CRG* 25:52, 24:434–35.
23. Ibid., 24:435–36.
24. Ibid., 24:436–40.
25. Fogleman, *Hopeful Journeys*; *CRG* 24:440–41.
26. *CRG* 24:441–43.
27. Ibid., 24:442–43; *Urlsperger* 11:25–26; Cashin, *Bethesda*, 68.
28. *CRG* 25:163–66; Peter Wood, "Slave Labor Camps in Early America: Overcoming Denial and Discovering the Gulag," in *Inequality in Early America*, ed. Pestana and Salinger, 222–38.
29. *CRG* 25:50–51.
30. Taylor, *Georgia Plan*, 226–27; *CRG* 6:156–57, 166, 169, 25:82–83, 88, 100–101. An observer remarked, "It's true Mr Harris Acquiesces in what his Partner has done, but we hear (by the by) that it was intirely owing to the Overbearing power that Mr Habersham hath, which brought him to comply."
31. *CRG* 6:171–78, 183, 192, 195–203, 207–8; Kars, *Breaking Loose Together*.
32. *CRG* 25:36–37, 66, 233, 6:332–33.
33. Ibid., 25:68, 200–213; *Urlsperger* 11:12–13, 44–45.
34. Ivers, *British Drums*, 202.
35. *Urlsperger* 11:75.
36. *CRG* 25:236–37, 291–95.

37. Ibid., 25:163–66, 279–86, 395, 6:230, 249, 26:4.

38. Ibid., 25:347; *Urlsperger* 12:101.

39. *CRG* 25:347–51. Within five years, Georgia had adopted Carolina's slave code. Pressly, *On the Rim*, 150.

40. *CRG* 25:371, 385.

41. Lambert, *Habersham*, 1, 130–31.

Chapter Six

1. *CRG* 6:254.

2. Ibid., 6:253–68.

3. Ibid., 6:278–85.

4. Ibid., 26:493–94, 499. Some historians have ignored these claims, despite the corroborating evidence that no hostility actually came about and the regiment had just left to Habersham's dismay (*CRG* 25:397–401). But a recent work, Juricek, *Colonial Georgia and the Creeks*, explains the incident much more fully and from Thomas Bosomworth's perspective. The unfolding of the incident according to the Board documentation makes less sense than the affidavits. Later records indicate that the Board officials were taking control away from the elderly Stephens (*CRG* 6:332–33), clarifying that the tension portrayed in the Board meeting records all came from the pen of Habersham, within a week of his taking his place on the Board.

5. *CRG* 25:417.

6. Sweet, *William Stephens*, 174. St. Catherines is now owned by a private foundation, mostly serving scientific endeavors, including lemur preservation.

7. *CRG* 7:133, 170–71; Pressly's *On the Rim* marvelously depicts the Royal era as Georgia's planters and merchants joined the economic system of the West Indies.

8. *CRG* 6:192–99, 224–26, 229, 301, 304, 369–72.

9. Chesnutt, *South Carolina's Expansion*, 51–60; Gallay, *Formation of a Planter Elite*, 29, 90–91.

10. Coleman, *Colonial Georgia*, 223–24.

11. *CRG* 7:64–66, 94–95, 100, 218, 252, 255, 283–85.

12. Gallay, *Formation of a Planter Elite*, 67–71; Lambert, *Habersham*, 1; Smith, *Slavery and Rice Culture*, 4–5.

13. Quoted in Lambert, *Habersham*, 139; Zacek, "West Indian Plantation Society," in Middleton and Smith, *Class Matters*, 75.

14. Moll gives the standard excuse for taking from someone else that which she had craved her whole life: personal and economic autonomy.

15. Bolzius, "Reliable Answer," 228–29, 237.

16. Loewald et al., "Questionnaire," 232, 236–40, 243, 250; poem quoted in Louis De Vorsey Jr., "The Colonial Georgia Backcountry," in *Colonial Augusta*, ed. Edward J. Cashin, 23.

17. Loewald et al., "Questionnaire," 231, 246–48; Davis, *Fledgling Province*, 33–44, 80; Glassie, *Patterns in Material Folk Culture*, 64–83; Jordan and Kaups, *American Backwoods Frontier*, 179–87.

18. Bolzius, "Reliable Answer," 229, 242; Loewald et al., "Questionnaire," 234–35.

19. *WSJ* 4:175; Bolzius, "Reliable Answer," 239–40; *CRG* 7:137–38; McNeill, *Mosquito Empires*, 71.

20. McNeill, *Mosquito Empires*, 53; *Urlsperger* 12:53, 58, 78, 97.

21. *Urlsperger* 11:2, 85–88, 12:2–4, 20, 30, 33, 54, 95–96.

22. Lockley, *Lines in the Sand*, 27; Bolzius, "Reliable Answer," 244.

23. *Urlsperger* 11:4, 108.

24. Bolzius, "Reliable Answer," 232, 240, 243; Davis, *Fledgling Province*, 51–56.

25. Loewald et al., "Questionnaire," 232–35, 246; Bolzius, "Reliable Answer," 253; Bonner, "Silk Growing," 146–47.

26. Bolzius, "Reliable Answer," 251–53; Loewald et al., "Questionnaire," 243; Helen Callahan, "Colonial Life in Augusta," in *Colonial Augusta*, ed. Edward J. Cashin, 117; Pressly, *On the Rim*, 193–208.

27. Loewald et al., "Questionnaire," 246–47; Lockley, *Lines in the Sand*, 11–13; quotation from Melton, "Alpine Miner," 126.

28. Bolzius, "Reliable Answer," 233–34, 236, 256; Pressly, *On the Rim*, 112–31. See also Morgan, *Slave Counterpoint*, 590 for accounts of suicide.

29. Bolzius, "Reliable Answer," 235–36, 257–59; Chaplin, *Anxious Pursuit*, 138, 251–52; Morgan, "Work and Culture," 563–99; Pressly, *On the Rim*, 148.

30. Loewald et al., "Questionnaire," 240; Morgan, "Work and Culture," 572–75. Besides, the same kind of descriptors would be applied to poor whites behind their backs in the decades before and afterward. Race science ballooned in the mid-nineteenth century, fashioning a supposedly empirical and distressingly long-lived framework for global expansion by white supremacists, but many who would adopt that worldview ignored the fine print of the "science." Samuel Morton busied himself measuring skulls of every population, not merely a general Caucasian versus a general Negro. He composed a scale within white ethnicities, with the Irish at the bottom, barely human, according to Morton. Morton, *Crania Americana*.

31. Smith, *Slavery and Rice Culture*, 20; Reese, *Colonial Georgia*, 48. Spalding, *Oglethorpe in America*, 74, however, contests notions of slavery's inevitability and whether "the pattern of southern colonial slaveholding might have been dramatically broken."

32. Williams, *Country and the City*, 37, 105–6.

33. Migliazzo, *To Make This Land Our Own*, 46.

34. Ibid., 92–95, 153; McNeill, *Mosquito Empires*, 104.

35. Migliazzo, *To Make This Land Our Own*, 178–81, 189–93.

36. Ibid., 193–95, 202.

37. Ibid., 206–27; Chaplin, *Anxious Pursuit*, 171.

38. Lockley, *Lines in the Sand*, 21–28. Michele Gillespie's excellent work, *Free Labor in an Unfree World*, carries the examination of class into the nineteenth century.

39. Lockley, *Lines in the Sand*, 167; Gallay, *Formation of a Planter Elite*, 164.

40. Reese, *Colonial Georgia*, 38, 44–45, 113–14; Pressly, *On the Rim*, 211.

41. Illick, *Colonial Pennsylvania*, 113, 123.

42. Smolenski, *Friends and Strangers*, 106, 215.

43. Pennsylvania's farmers did not achieve the degree of equality they sought, of course. See Bouton's *Taming Democracy*.

44. Ulrich, *Midwife's Tale*.

45. Lane, *General Oglethorpe's Georgia,* 2:398; Morgan, *Slave Counterpoint,* 35–40.

46. Fogleman, *Hopeful Journeys,* 18–31, 73.

47. *CRG* 20:75, 120–21; Bolzius, "Reliable Answer," 226–27.

48. Bolzius, "Reliable Answer," 235–37, 245; Morgan, *Slave Counterpoint,* 38.

49. Migliazzo, *Make This Land Our Own,* 205.

Conclusion

1. Bolzius, "Reliable Answer," 251; Melton, "Alpine Miner," 135, 138.

Bibliography

Unpublished Primary Sources

Athens, Ga.
    Egmont Papers 14210, Hargrett Rare Books and Manuscripts Library,
        University of Georgia
Savannah, Ga.
    Habersham Family Papers, Collections of the Georgia Historical Society
Charleston, S.C.
    William R. Coe Collection, South Carolina Historical Society
London, U.K.
    Colonial Office, British National Archives

Published Primary Sources

Bolzius, Johann Martin. "Reliable Answer to Some Submitted Questions
    Concerning the Land Carolina." *William and Mary Quarterly,* 3rd ser., 14 (Apr.
    1957): 223–61.
Candler, Allen D. et al., eds. *The Colonial Records of the State of Georgia.* Vols. 1–19,
    21–26. Atlanta: Franklin Printing, 1904–16.
Coleman, Kenneth, and Milton Ready, eds. *The Colonial Records of the State of
    Georgia: Original Papers, Correspondence to the Trustees, James Oglethorpe, and
    Others, 1732–1735.* Vol. 20. Athens: University of Georgia Press, 1982.
——. *The Colonial Records of the State of Georgia: Trustees' Letter Book, 1732–1738.*
    Vol. 29. Athens: University of Georgia Press, 1985.
Coulter, E. Merton, and Albert B. Saye, eds. *A List of the Early Settlers of Georgia.*
    Athens: University of Georgia Press, 1949.
Curnock, Nehemiah, ed. *John Wesley's Journal.* London: Epworth Press 1938.
Fleming, Berry. *Autobiography of a Colony: The First Half-Century of Augusta,
    Georgia.* Athens: University of Georgia Press, 1957.
Fortson, Ben W., and Pat Bryant. *Entry of Claims for Georgia Landholders,
    1733–1755.* Atlanta: State Printing Office, 1975.
Gallay, Alan, ed. *Voices of the Old South: Eyewitness Accounts, 1528–1861.* Athens:
    University of Georgia Press, 1994.
Gillies, John, ed. *Memoirs of Rev. George Whitefield.* Middletown, Conn.: Hunt and
    Noyes, 1837.
Gordon, Peter. *The Journal of Peter Gordon.* Edited by E. Merton Coulter. Athens:
    University of Georgia Press, 1963.

Jones, George F., and Renate Wilson, eds. *Detailed Reports on the Salzburger Emigrants Who Settled in America, Edited by Samuel Urlsperger*. Vols. 6–12, 1739–48. Athens: University of Georgia Press, 1981.

Killpatrick, James. *An Impartial Account of the Late Expedition against St. Augustine under General Oglethorpe, 1742*. Gainesville: University Press of Florida, 1978.

Kimber, Edward. *A Relation or Journal of a Late Expedition*. Gainesville: University Press of Florida, 1976.

Lane, Mills, ed. *General Oglethorpe's Georgia: Colonial Letters, 1733–1743*. 2 vols. Savannah: Beehive Press, 1975.

Loewald, Klaus G., Beverly Starika, Paul S. Taylor, and Johann M. Bolzius. "Johann Martin Bolzius Answers a Questionnaire on Carolina and Georgia: Part II." *William and Mary Quarterly*, 3rd ser., 15 (Apr. 1958): 228–52.

McPherson, Robert, ed. *Journal of the Earl of Egmont: Abstract of the Trustees Proceedings for Establishing the Colony of Georgia, 1732–38*. Athens: University of Georgia Press, 1962.

Morton, Samuel George. *Crania Americana*. Philadelphia: J. Dobson, 1839.

Reese, Trevor, ed. *The Clamorous Malcontents: Criticisms and Defenses of the Colony of Georgia, 1741–1743*. Savannah: Beehive Press, 1973.

———. *The Most Delightful Country of the Universe: Promotional Literature of the Colony of Georgia, 1717–1734*. Savannah: Beehive Press, 1972.

Salley, Alexander S., ed. *Narratives of Early Carolina, 1650–1708*. New York: Charles Scribner's Sons, 1911.

Smith, Mark M., ed. *Stono: Documenting and Interpreting a Southern Slave Revolt*. Columbia: University of South Carolina Press, 2005.

Stephens, William. *A Journal of the Proceedings in Georgia*. Edited by E. Merton Coulter. 2 vols., 1741–43, 1743–45. Athens: University of Georgia Press, 1958–59.

———. *A Journal of the Proceedings in Georgia*. Vols. 1–2. New York: Readex Microprint Corporation, 1966.

Wesley, John. *The Journal of the Rev. John Wesley AM in 4 Volumes*. Vol. 1. London: J. M. Dent & Sons, 1906.

Whitefield, George. *George Whitefield's Journals*. Lafayette, Ind.: Sovereign Grace Publishers, 2000.

———. *George Whitefield's Letters, 1734–1742*. Edinburgh: Banner of Truth Trust, 1976.

Secondary Sources

Baine, Rodney M. "Myths of Mary Musgrove." *Georgia Historical Quarterly* 76 (Summer 1992): 428–35.

Bannon, John F. *The Spanish Borderlands Frontier, 1513–1821*. Albuquerque: University of New Mexico Press, 1974.

Beattie, J. M. *Policing and Punishment in London, 1660–1750: Urban Crime and the Limits of Terror*. Oxford: Oxford University Press, 2001.

Berlin, Ira. *Many Thousands Gone: The First Two Centuries of Slavery in North America*. Cambridge: Harvard University Press, 1998.

Bonner, James. "Silk Growing in the Georgia Colony." *Agricultural History* 43 (Jan. 1969): 143–48.

Bonomi, Patricia. *Under the Cope of Heaven: Religion, Society, and Politics in Colonial America.* New York: Oxford University Press, 1986.

Bouton, Terry. *Taming Democracy: "The People," the Founders, and the Troubled Ending of the American Revolution.* New York: Oxford University Press, 2007.

Braund, Kathryn Holland. *Deerskins and Duffels: The Creek Indian Trade with Anglo-Americans, 1685-1815.* Lincoln: University of Nebraska Press, 2008.

Brewer, Holly. *By Birth or Consent: Children, Law, and the Anglo-American Revolution in Authority.* Chapel Hill: University of North Carolina Press, 2005.

Brundage, Anthony. *The English Poor Laws, 1700-1930.* London: Palgrave Macmillan, 2001.

Butler, Jon. "Enthusiasm Described and Decried: The Great Awakening as Interpretative Fiction." *Journal of American History* 69 (Sept. 1982): 305–25.

Carp, Benjamin L. *Rebels Rising: Cities and the American Revolution.* New York: Oxford University Press, 2007.

Cashin, Edward J. *Beloved Bethesda: A History of George Whitefield's Home for Boys, 1740-2000.* Macon, Ga.: Mercer University Press, 2001.

———. *Guardians of the Valley: The Chickasaws in Colonial South Carolina and Georgia.* Columbia: University of South Carolina Press, 2008.

———, ed. *Colonial Augusta, "Key of the Indian Countrey."* Macon, Ga.: Mercer University Press, 1986.

Cates, Gerald L. "The Seasoning: Disease and Death among the First Colonists of Georgia." *Georgia Historical Quarterly* 64 (Summer 1980): 146–58.

Chaplin, Joyce E. *An Anxious Pursuit: Agricultural Innovation and Modernity in the Lower South, 1730-1815.* Chapel Hill: University of North Carolina Press, 1993.

Chesnutt, David R. *South Carolina's Expansion into Colonial Georgia, 1720-1765.* New York: Garland, 1989.

Clinton, Catherine, and Michele Gillespie, eds. *The Devil's Lane: Sex and Race in the Early South.* New York: Oxford University Press, 1997.

Coleman, Kenneth. *Colonial Georgia: A History.* New York: Charles Scribner's Sons, 1967.

———. "The Southern Frontier: Georgia's Founding and the Expansion of South Carolina." *Georgia Historical Quarterly* 56 (Summer 1972): 163–74.

Crawford, Michael J. *Seasons of Grace: Colonial New England's Revival Tradition in its British Context.* New York: Oxford University Press, 1991.

Dalliamore, Arnold. *George Whitefield: The Life and Times of the Great Evangelist of the Eighteenth-Century Revival.* Vol. 1. Edinburgh: Banner of Truth Trust, 1970.

Davis, Harold. *The Fledgling Province: Social and Cultural Life in Colonial Georgia, 1733-1776.* Chapel Hill: University of North Carolina Press, 1976.

Davis, Mollie C. "Deference or Defiance in Eighteenth Century America: A Round Table." *Journal of American History* 85 (June 1998): 13–97.

Defoe, Daniel. *Moll Flanders: An Authoritative Text, Contexts, Criticism.* Edited by Albert Rivero. New York: W. W. Norton, 2004.

Ekirch, A. Roger. *Bound for America: The Transportation of British Convicts to the Colonies, 1718-1775*. New York: Oxford University Press, 1987.

Eltis, David, Philip Morgan, and David Richardson. "Black, Brown, or White? Color-Coding American Commercial Rice Cultivation with Slave Labor." *American Historical Review* 115 (Feb. 2010): 164–71.

Ettinger, Amos. *Oglethorpe: A Brief Biography*. Macon, Ga.: Mercer University Press, 1984.

Fletcher, Anthony, and John Stevenson, eds. *Order and Disorder in Early Modern England*. Cambridge: Cambridge University Press, 1985.

Fogleman, Aaron. *Hopeful Journeys: German Immigration, Settlement, and Political Culture in Colonial America, 1717-1775*. Philadelphia: University of Pennsylvania Press, 1996.

Fraser, Walter J. *Savannah in the Old South*. Athens: University of Georgia Press, 2003.

Galenson, David. *White Servitude in Colonial America: An Economic Analysis*. New York: Cambridge University Press, 1981.

Gallay, Alan. *The Formation of A Planter Elite: Jonathan Bryan and the Southern Colonial Frontier*. Athens: University of Georgia Press, 1989.

——. *The Indian Slave Trade: The Rise of the English Empire in the American South, 1670-1717*. New Haven, Conn.: Yale University Press, 2002.

——. "The Origins of Slaveholders' Paternalism: George Whitefield, the Bryan Family, and the Great Awakening in the South." *Journal of Southern History* 53 (Aug. 1987): 369–94.

Gaustad, Edwin S. *The Great Awakening in New England*. Gloucester, Mass.: Peter Smith, 1965.

Gillespie, Michele. *Free Labor in an Unfree World: White Artisans in Slaveholding Georgia, 1789-1860*. Athens: University of Georgia Press, 2000.

Glassie, Henry. *Patterns in the Material Folk Culture of the Eastern United States*. Philadelphia: University of Pennsylvania Press, 1971.

Greene, Jack P., Rosemary Brana-Shute, and Randy J. Sparks, eds. *Money, Trade, and Power: The Evolution of Colonial South Carolina's Plantation Society*. Columbia: University of South Carolina Press, 2001.

Gura, Philip F. *Jonathan Edwards: America's Evangelical*. New York: Hill and Wang, 2005.

Hahn, Steven. *The Life and Times of Mary Musgrove*. Gainesville: University Press of Florida, 2012.

Hall, Timothy. *Contested Boundaries: Itinerancy and the Reshaping of the Colonial American Religious World*. Durham, N.C.: Duke University Press, 1994.

Hattersley, Roy. *The Life of John Wesley: A Brand from the Burning*. New York: Doubleday, 2003.

Hempton, David. *Methodism, Empire of the Spirit*. New Haven, Conn.: Yale University Press, 2005.

Hoffer, Peter Charles. *Cry Liberty: The Great Stono River Slave Rebellion of 1739*. New York: Oxford University Press, 2012.

————. *When Benjamin Franklin Met the Reverend Whitefield: Enlightenment, Revival, and the Power of the Printed Word.* Baltimore: Johns Hopkins University Press, 2011.

Hoffman, Ronald, Mechal Sobel, and Fredrika J. Teinte, eds. *Through a Glass Darkly: Reflections on Personal Identity in Early America.* Chapel Hill: University of North Carolina Press, 1997.

Illick, Joseph E. *Colonial Pennsylvania: A History.* New York: Charles Scribner's Sons, 1976.

Inscoe, John, ed. *James Edward Oglethorpe: New Perspectives on His Life and Legacy.* Savannah: Georgia Historical Society, 1997.

Isaac, Rhys. "Evangelical Revolt: The Nature of the Baptists' Challenge to the Traditional Order in Virginia, 1765 to 1775." *William and Mary Quarterly,* 3rd ser., 31 (July 1974): 345–68.

Ivers, Larry E. "The Battle of Fort Mosa." *Georgia Historical Quarterly* 51 (June 1967): 135–53.

————. *British Drums on the Southern Frontier: The Military Colonization of Georgia, 1733–1749.* Chapel Hill: University of North Carolina Press, 1974.

Jackson, Harvey H. "The Carolina Connection: Jonathan Bryan, His Brothers, and the Founding of Georgia, 1733–1752." *Georgia Historical Quarterly* 68 (Summer 1984): 147–72.

————. "The Darien Antislavery Petition of 1739 and the Georgia Plan." *William and Mary Quarterly,* 3rd ser., 34 (Oct. 1977): 618–31.

————. "Hugh Bryan and the Evangelical Movement in Colonial South Carolina." *William and Mary Quarterly,* 3rd ser., 43 (Oct. 1986): 594–614.

Jackson, Harvey L., and Phinzy Spaulding, eds. *Forty Years of Diversity: Essays on Colonial Georgia.* Athens: University of Georgia Press, 1984.

Jones, George Fenwick. *The Georgia Dutch: From the Rhine and Danube to the Savannah, 1733–1783.* Athens: University of Georgia Press, 1992.

————. *The Salzburger Saga: Religious Exiles and Other Germans along the Savannah.* Athens: University of Georgia Press, 1984.

Jordan, Terry G., and Matti Kaups. *The American Backwoods Frontier: An Ethnic and Ecological Interpretation.* Baltimore: John Hopkins University Press, 1989.

Juricek, John. *Colonial Georgia and the Creeks: Anglo-Indian Diplomacy on the Southern Frontier, 1733–1763.* Gainesville: University Press of Florida, 2010.

Kars, Marjoleine. *Breaking Loose Together: The Regulator Rebellion in Pre-Revolutionary North Carolina.* Chapel Hill: University of North Carolina Press, 2001.

Kidd, Thomas S. *The Great Awakening: The Roots of Evangelical Christianity in Colonial America.* New Haven, Conn.: Yale University Press, 2007.

Kulikoff, Allan. *From British Peasants to Colonial American Farmers.* Chapel Hill: University of North Carolina Press, 2000.

Kussmaul, Ann. *Servants in Husbandry in Early Modern England.* New York: Cambridge University Press, 1981.

Lambert, Frank. *James Habersham: Loyalty, Politics, and Commerce in Colonial Georgia*. Athens: University of Georgia Press, 2005.

——. *Pedlar in Divinity: George Whitefield and the Transatlantic Revivals*. Princeton, N.J.: Princeton University Press, 1994.

Landers, Jane. *Black Society in Spanish Florida*. Urbana: University of Illinois Press, 1999.

Landsman, Ned C. *Scotland and Its First American Colony, 1683-1765*. Princeton, N.J.: Princeton University Press, 1985.

Linebaugh, Peter. *The London Hanged: Crime and Civil Society in the Eighteenth Century*. New York: Cambridge University Press, 1992.

Lockley, Timothy James. *Lines in the Sand: Race and Class in Lowcountry Georgia, 1750-1860*. Athens: University of Georgia Press, 2001.

Marsh, Ben. *Georgia's Frontier Women: Female Fortunes in a Southern Colony*. Athens: University of Georgia Press, 2007.

Mathias, Peter. *The Transformation of England: Essays in the Economic and Social History of England in the Eighteenth Century*. New York: Columbia University Press, 1979.

McCusker, John J., and Russell R. Menard. *The Economy of British America, 1607-1789*. Chapel Hill: University of North Carolina Press, 1985.

McGowen, Randall. "The Well-Ordered Prison: England, 1780-1865." In *The Oxford History of the Prison: The Practice of Punishment in Western Society*. Edited by Norval Morris and David Rothman. New York: Oxford University Press, 1995.

McIlvenna, Noeleen. *A Very Mutinous People: The Struggle for North Carolina, 1660-1713*. Chapel Hill: University of North Carolina Press, 2009.

McNeill, J. R. *Mosquito Empires: Ecology and War in the Greater Caribbean, 1620-1914*. New York: Cambridge University Press, 2010.

Melton, James. "From Alpine Miner to Lowcountry Yeoman: Transatlantic Worlds of a Georgia Salzburger, 1693-1761." *Past and Present* 201 (Nov. 2008): 97-140.

Meroney, Geraldine. "The London Entrepot Merchants and the Georgia Colony." *William and Mary Quarterly*, 3rd ser., 25 (Apr. 1968): 230-44.

Merrell, James H. *The Indians' New World: Catawbas and Their Neighbors from European Contact through the Era of Removal*. Chapel Hill: University of North Carolina Press, 1989.

Middleton, Simon, and Billy Smith, eds. *Class Matters: Early North America and the Atlantic World*. Philadelphia: University of Pennsylvania Press, 2008.

Migliazzo, Arlin C. *To Make This Land Our Own: Community, Identity, and Cultural Adaptation in Purrysburg Township, South Carolina, 1732-1865*. Columbia: University of South Carolina Press, 2007.

Morgan, David T. "The Consequences of George Whitefield's Ministry in the Carolinas and Georgia, 1739-40." *Georgia Historical Quarterly* 55 (Spring 1971): 62-82.

——. "Judaism in Eighteenth Century Georgia." *Georgia Historical Quarterly* 58 (Spring 1974): 41-54.

Morgan, Philip D. *Slave Counterpoint: Black Culture in the Eighteenth-Century Chesapeake and Lowcountry*. Chapel Hill: University of North Carolina Press, 1998.

———. "Work and Culture: The Task System and the World of Lowcountry Blacks, 1700 to 1880." *William and Mary Quarterly*, 3rd ser., 39 (Oct. 1982): 563–99.

Morris, Norval, and David Rothman, eds. *The Oxford History of the Prison: The Practice of Punishment in Western Society*. New York: Oxford University Press, 1995.

Noll, Mark. *The Rise of Evangelicalism: The Age of Edwards, Whitefield and the Wesleys*. Downers Grove, Ill.: InterVarsity Press, 2003.

Olwell, Robert. *Masters, Slaves, and Subjects: The Culture of Power in the South Carolina Low Country, 1740–1790*. Ithaca, N.Y.: Cornell University Press, 1988.

Parent, Anthony. *Foul Means: The Formation of a Slave Society in Virginia, 1660–1740*. Chapel Hill: University of North Carolina Press, 2003.

Parker, Anthony. *Scottish Highlanders in Colonial Georgia: The Recruitment, Emigration and Settlement at Darien, 1735–48*. Athens: University of Georgia Press, 1997.

Pennington, Edgar Legare. "John Wesley's Georgia Ministry." *Church History* 8 (Sept. 1939): 231–54.

Pestana, Carla Gardina, and Sharon V. Salinger, eds. *Inequality in Early America*. Hanover, N.H.: University Press of New England, 1999.

Pressly, Paul. *On the Rim of the Caribbean: Colonial Georgia and the British Atlantic World*. Athens: University of Georgia Press, 2013.

Proctor, Samuel, ed. *Eighteenth-Century Florida and its Borderlands*. Gainesville: University Press of Florida, 1975.

Reese, Trevor R. *Colonial Georgia: A Study in British Imperial Policy in the Eighteenth Century*. Athens: University of Georgia Press, 1963.

———. "Georgia in Anglo-Spanish Diplomacy, 1736–1739." *William and Mary Quarterly*, 3rd ser., 15 (Apr. 1958): 168–90.

Reynes, Genevieve. *Couvent de femmes: La vie des religieuses contemplatives dans la France des XVIIe et XVIIIe siecles*. Paris: Fayard, 1987.

Rucker, Walter C. *The River Flows On: Black Resistance, Culture and Identity Formation in Early America*. Baton Rouge: Louisiana State University Press, 2006.

Russell, David Lee. *Oglethorpe and Colonial Georgia: A History, 1733–1783*. Jefferson, N.C.: McFarland, 2006.

Silver, Timothy. *A New Face on the Countryside: Indians, Colonists, and Slaves in South Atlantic Forests, 1500–1800*. New York: Cambridge University Press, 1990.

Smith, Abbot Emerson. *Colonists in Bondage: White Servitude and Convict Labor in America, 1607–1776*. New York: Norton, 1975.

Smith, Julia Floyd. *Slavery and Rice Culture in Low Country Georgia, 1750–1860*. Knoxville: University of Tennessee Press, 1985.

Smolenski, John. *Friends and Strangers: The Making of a Creole Culture in Colonial Pennsylvania*. Philadelphia: University of Pennsylvania Press, 2010.

Spalding, Phinizy. *Oglethorpe in America*. Chicago: University of Chicago Press, 1977.

Stark, Rodney. *For the Glory of God: How Monotheism Led to Reformations, Science, Witch-Hunts, and the End of Slavery*. Princeton, N.J.: Princeton University Press, 2003.

Stein, Stephen J. "George Whitefield on Slavery: Some New Evidence." *Church History* 42 (June 1973): 243–56.

Stewart, Mart A. *What Nature Suffers to Groe: Life, Labor, and Landscape on the Georgia Coast, 1680–1920*. Athens: University of Georgia Press, 1996.

Stout, Harry S. *The Divine Dramatist: George Whitefield and the Rise of Modern Evangelicalism*. Grand Rapids, Mich.: William B. Eerdmans Publishing Company, 1991.

Sturgill, Claude C., and E. R. Turner. "The Importance of Being at War: General James Oglethorpe's Accounts and Imperial Affairs in Early Colonial Georgia." *Military Affairs* 40 (Oct. 1976): 129–35.

Sweet, Julie Anne. "A Misguided Mistake: The Trustees' Public Garden in Savannah, Georgia." *Georgia Historical Quarterly* 93 (Spring 2009): 1–29.

———. "The Murder of William Wise: An Examination of Indentured Servitude, Anti-Irish Prejudice, and Crime in Early Georgia." *Georgia Historical Quarterly* 96 (Spring 2012): 1–23.

———. *Negotiating for Georgia: British-Creek Relations in the Trustee Era, 1733–1752*. Athens: University of Georgia Press, 2005.

———. "The Thirteenth Colony in Perspective: Historians' Views on Early Georgia." *Georgia Historical Quarterly* 85 (Fall 2001): 435–60.

———. *William Stephens: Georgia's Forgotten Founder*. Baton Rouge: Louisiana State University Press, 2010.

Taylor, Paul S. *Georgia Plan: 1732–1752*. Berkeley: Institute of Business and Economic Research, 1972.

Temple, Sarah, and Kenneth Coleman. *Georgia Journeys*. Athens: University of Georgia Press, 1961.

Thomas, Hugh. *The Slave Trade: The Story of the Atlantic Slave Trade, 1440–1870*. New York: Simon and Schuster, 1997.

Thomas, J. E. *House of Care: Prisons and Prisoners in England, 1500–1800*. Nottingham, U.K.: University of Nottingham, 1988.

Thompson, E. P. *Customs in Common*. New York: New Press, 1991.

———. *The Making of the English Working Class*. New York: Vintage Books, 1966.

———. *Whigs and Hunters: The Origin of the Black Act*. New York: Pantheon Books, 1975.

Thornton, John K. "African Dimensions of the Stono Rebellion." *American Historical Review* 96 (October 1991): 1101–13.

Todd, Helen. *Mary Musgrove: Georgia Indian Princess*. Chicago: Seven Oaks, 1981.

Ulrich, Laurel Thatcher. *A Midwife's Tale: The Life of Martha Ballard, Based on Her Diary, 1785–1812*. New York: Vintage, 1991.

Waselkov, Gregory, Peter H. Wood, and M. Thomas Hatley, eds. *Powhatan's Mantle: Indians in the Colonial Southeast*. Lincoln: University of Nebraska Press, 2006.

Weeks, Carl S. *Savannah in the Time of Peter Tondee*. Columbia, S.C.: Summerhouse Press, 1997.

Weir, Robert M. *Colonial South Carolina: A History*. New York: KTO Press, 1983.

Williams, Raymond. *The Country and the City*. New York: Oxford University Press, 1973.

Wood, Betty. *Slavery in Colonial Georgia, 1730–1775*. Athens: University of Georgia Press, 1984.

Wood, Bradford J. *This Remote Part of the World: Regional Formation in Lower Cape Fear, North Carolina, 1725–1775*. Columbia: University of South Carolina Press, 2004.

Wood, Peter H. *Black Majority: Negroes in Colonial South Carolina from 1670 through the Stono Rebellion*. New York: Knopf, 1974.

UNPUBLISHED PHD DISSERTATIONS

Cates, Gerald L. "A Medical History of Georgia: The First Hundred Years, 1733–1833." University of Georgia, 1976.

Lannen, Andrew. "Liberty and Authority in Colonial Georgia, 1717–1776." Louisiana State University, 2002.

Rabac, Donna Marie. "Economy and Society in Early Georgia: A Functional Analysis of the Colony's Origins and Evolution." University of Michigan, 1978.

Ready, Milton. "An Economic History of Colonial Georgia." University of Georgia, 1970.

Index